MORTAL MORALS

FOR FINANCIAL WELL BEING

SANDEEP GHAG

notionpress.com

INDIA • SINGAPORE • MALAYSIA

ISBN 979-8-89544-844-1

Contents

Foreword

In an increasingly material world, driven by ambition to pursue financial well-being as an ultimate goal for happiness, we often forget a key element that determines our success – the mortal morals. 'Mortal Morals' is a book that closes this gap, inviting you to reflect upon how ethical foundations play a role not only in your life, but also in shaping your financial destiny.

This book is more than just a roadmap to financial success. It signals the reader inwards, to self-reflect, examine the values that drive us, and explore the intimate relationship between our moral choices and our capacity to become truly financially free. With powerful stories, practical wisdom and an exploration into the very fabric of morality itself, 'Mortal Morals' leads readers on a path to financial wellness as it was meant to be – steeped in deep integrity.

Having coached people for over a decade on the path to financial freedom, I've learned that wealth alone – pursued without a moral compass – breeds empty results. Financial freedom is not just about money; it's about creating a life of meaning, contribution, and enduring fulfillment. This book represents that reality.

My hope is that this book will encourage you to take another look inside yourself, re-evaluate what's important to you in your life, and match your financial goals with whatever unique moral beliefs you hold. May it be a road map for you, a friend by your side, and a place of knowledge.

"To educate a person in the mind but not in morals is to educate a menace to society."

— Theodore Roosevelt

About Me

Born in a world where barriers and challenges were a cornerstone; I was instilled with the courage to confront those barriers. My parents, both blind, not just tested me with limited means for a family income, but also filled me with persistence and determination. My school, (St. Francis D'Assisi High School, Borivali West) sponsored my education hence opportunities were presented which helped me foresee beyond our situation.

When I was just 13, tragedy struck. My father fell terribly ill and for the next seven years of my life I had to take on responsibilities many people my age, were not familiar with (and shouldn't be, either). Life was tough but it was during this time that I learnt what true resilience meant.

From 1998 to 1999, I worked as a delivery person for a dry cleaner. I was paid ₹300 per month (yes, you read it right — ₹10 per day). Then in 2000, I joined a Chartered Accountant's office where I started earning ₹1,500 per month. In the same year, I became an assistant of a Development Officer at LIC and my salary grew up to ₹2,500 per month. These were tough jobs but helped me become more resolute about achieving financial well-being.

Breaking into corporate wasn't an easy feat either. After 36 interviews, I finally landed my first BPO job in the year 2003. (No, that's not a typo – it took 36 interviews to embark on my corporate journey.)

In 2012, after nine long years of my career I began the journey of saving money. It's never **TOO LATE**. one of the things we did as part of our future building plan, was that my wife Komal and I decided we won't have a meal outside home for next 3 years, and we didn't.

Not one dream I ever had was easy but love, determination and an unbreakable desire to work hard and live with integrity has been my moral compass. I am proud of the life Komal and I have built and the togetherness we have nurtured. Whatever I'm destined to do in the years ahead, I will give my all. It's never been easy but as I said before, the drive has never been more alive!

From financial hardship to personal adversity, each struggle taught me lessons that propelled me towards financial well-being. Rather than allowing those struggles to define me, I utilized them as the building blocks to create a solid foundation of morality and used the knowledge I gained from those experiences to help guide me towards financial well-being. With every ounce of determination and an infinite amount of discipline and preparation, I completely shifted my financial reality and am walking the path of achieving financial stability and independence.

That's why I've dedicated my spare time to creating a movement— **Uplift-India!**

At Uplift-India, we're on a mission to empower 1 Crore youth to create wealth, achieve financial success, and lead fulfilling lives. Our platform is dedicated to providing accessible financial education, coaching, and resources, especially for those from underprivileged backgrounds, to help them break free from financial constraints and build a prosperous future.

We envision a world where everyone, regardless of their educational or socio-economical background, can generate wealth and abundance. Learn more about our unique approach to financial empowerment, hear success stories from those we've helped, and discover how you too can be part of this transformative journey.

Whether you're looking to improve your financial literacy, need guidance on managing your money, or want to achieve your financial goals, Uplift-India is here to support you every step of the way.

Subscribe to our YouTube channel—@UpliftIndia—to stay updated on the latest tips, success stories, and motivational content that will help you take control of your financial future.

Visit our website: www.uplift-india.com to learn more and be a part of our movement.

"The world breaks everyone, and afterward, some are strong at the broken places."

— Ernest Hemingway

Introduction to the book

Financial well-being is often seen as a goal. The finish line. The point at which you've reached a level of wealth where you can live without money worries. But what if the journey is the destination? What if the way we reach financial freedom is just as important as our destination? What if our own personal principles become casualties in the fight to get there?

'Mortal Morals' is a product of these intricate questions. The book was written to challenge our views of wealth and success, and raise the question of whether having morals could mean becoming financially free. In a world where the end justifies the means 'Mortal Morals' suggests we go back to our roots. That true financial freedom isn't just about creating material abundance, but living in accordance with your deepest moral compass.

The link between morality and money is not obvious, but it is extremely important. Our moral values guide our decisions – what we earn, how we spend, where we save, why we invest. They also determine our relationship with money – our attitude towards it and how much of it we have (or want). In essence, our moral values determine how sustainable our financial success will be. A person with strong moral values (honesty, empathy, fairness) will probably make better decisions that lead to sustainable wealth. A person who compromises on these moral values might make more money in a shorter time-frame – but at the expense of mental peace or their relationships or even their own happiness.

This book is designed to be a roadmap of self-discovery and financial knowledge. The upcoming chapters will discuss particular virtues—honesty, integrity, responsibility, and others—and how those virtues tie into the concept of financial freedom. You will encounter pragmatic suggestions, stories based in reality, and introspective questions meant to guide you on your journey toward synchronizing your financial aspirations with your moral character.

'Mortal Morals' is not a book for people who want to be financially free. It is meant for anyone who thinks of wealth as a means and not as an end in itself. It is for those, who feel that success should never be measured by the size of one's bank balance alone but also by the kind of life one lives – with full integrity.

As you read through the pages, you will be encouraged to reflect deeply on your values, challenge your financial decisions and live life in a way that is congruent with your financial dreams and moral compass. In the process, you will realize that the journey to financial freedom is not just about amassing wealth, but about creating a life that is abundant in every sense of the word.

Welcome to 'Mortal Morals.' Your journey to financial well-being, guided by the light of your moral compass, begins here.

"Morality is the basis of things and truth is the substance of all morality."

— Mahatma Gandhi

My Perspective

First, thank you for picking up this book and deciding to explore the **introspective** genre. I know that not every book is for everyone, and that's okay. It's normal to sample different mindsets until you discover the ones that work for what you want to achieve.

As you read 'Mortal Morals,' I invite you to have an open mind. These are deeply personal insights and perspectives that I've gained from my own journey and combined it with a few pieces of market research. All I ask is that you see how you can best apply it in your life to make the most impact on your growth and happiness.

This book is potentially a deep soul tool for self-awareness and personal growth. To maximize your benefit while reading it, I offer you the following suggestions for diving deep into the teachings.

- **Be Open-Minded**: It is expected that you approach the materials with an open mind, even if some concepts may stretch what you believe. Embrace the growth from the chance to investigate new ideas and perspectives.
- **Set Intentions**: Before you start reading take a few moments to set some clear intentions of

what you would like to receive from this book, what moral values are you wanting to enhance or develop for yourself.

- **Read Actively**: Highlight, take notes, or journal as you read to engage with and make meaning from the text.
- **Reflect on Personal Values**: Every so often, reflect on how the ideas you read about fit with your own life. How might the things you learn apply to your daily experience?
- **Do the exercises**. Seriously. They've been specifically designed to not only help you grasp the material, but to grow personally as well.
- **Practice Mindfulness**: Stay present and focused as you read. Pay attention to any emotional responses or thoughts that come up for you and use them as a starting point for further contemplation.
- **Tell Someone**: Feel free to voice your opinions about the book to someone close or a family member who shares similar interests as you do. These discussions open up new perspectives and also help you grow in the understanding of the topic.
- **Revisit and Review**: Once you've completed the book, go back to the key passages or ideas that resonated with you. Think about how your

perspective has shifted, and return to the book on occasion to help reinforce what you've learned.

- **Practice Patience and Persistence**: Personal growth is a process that takes time and determination. Be patient with yourself as you integrate new realizations, implement changes, and form new habits. Stay committed to your personal growth, even if it gets tough at times or you don't see immediate results.

Additional Tips for an Effective Reading Experience:

- **Read When Refreshed**: Select a time of day when you are the most mentally alert and your mind is the freshest. A tired mind can skew your interpretation and understanding of the content.

- **Read a few pages daily**: It is better to read slowly than to race through a book. The target should be to complete the book in 7 to 10 days so that you can easily grasp an understanding on the concepts.

- **Keep a Pen Handy** to jot things down and do the exercises in writing as you read.

Morals – Why are we talking about it?

In finance we tend to think about strategies, investments, and the technical part of managing money. However, we often miss one crucial part – our morals. In my career as a Financial Coach and Mentor I have realised that our values and ethical beliefs are a foundational element when it comes to making financial decisions which work for us and our overall well-being. The goal of this book is to open the conversation on why talking about morals is so important in relation to financial well-being; how our values and ethical beliefs can impact us on such a deep level when it comes to making financial decisions; and how they shape our sense of empowerment around money.

We will be getting pretty deep so hold on, this introspection is really important to knowing yourself and what you truly want out of your financial journey.

When I ask my clients, "What does financial well-being mean to you?" I often get a blank look. Financial well-being can feel like an abstract concept, and something that is difficult to define. It's not because people aren't financially literate. It's because their definition of what it means – is a moral one.

It's the moral frameworks through which we view money, success, and financial responsibility. Some people are driven by their morals to accumulate money for the reassurance of security and philanthropy; for others, it means being cautious or even sacrificing money because of ethical concerns.

The real challenge is when our morals don't line up with our financial goals. And, that's when we're dissatisfied, frustrated, or even feel 'stuck.' To achieve healthy financial well-being, it's important that we recognize how much our values impact our financial situation.

Sounds familiar? Ever been is this situation?

This is why I wrote this book — not to oversimplify money, but to simplify the process of thinking about financial well-being. And it all starts with a deeper look at our morals. By reflecting on our values, we can gain some insight into why we really do what we do with money — the unconscious motivations that drive our financial behavior and life choices. This awareness then equips us to better design our financial systems and processes in a way consistent with who we are and what's important — ultimately leading to more fulfilling results.

The main goal of this book is to help you understand and develop your own set of values and to show you how to apply those values in making financial decisions. When you know with certainty the kind of life you want to lead and the things that are important to you, it becomes easy to make decisions about money. The process I am going to describe in these pages will make all areas of financial planning less complex by helping you focus only on those things that will enhance your individual search for happiness.

In the chapters ahead, we will consider different dimensions of financial well-being from the perspective of moral self-examination. Our objective is to help you become more aware of the basic commitments that define your financial existence and that will be necessary for you to embrace if you hope to achieve genuine financial freedom.

Defining Morals!

Morals are the usual standards of behavior that enable people to live cooperatively in groups. Moral refers to what societies approve as right and acceptable. Most people tend to act morally and follow social guidelines. Morality describes the particular values of a specific group at a specific point in time. The term "moral" is derived from a Latin word "mos" (plural "mores") which means customs, conventions, habits, or rules.

Morals tell us what is right or wrong from the perspective of individuals and communities. Morals are the rules that govern which actions are right and which are wrong. Individual's morals are particular to themselves and can be influenced by many factors, including their personal beliefs, culture, religion, or law. "What directed our morals?" We can think that natural selected our moral sense by rewarding some behaviors and punishing others in our ancestral environment.

Moral codes differ among different people the cultures, religions or even personal beliefs. The justification of what is morally right or wrong could be culturally bound. What might be considered a moral action in one society could be quite different in another society.

Think of moral as your personal code of conduct; they are the set of rules you go by because you feel they are important. They help us to depict what is right and what is wrong. These rules can be from your upbringing, religion, culture, or experiences you have had in life. For instance, honesty, being nice to others, and taking care of each other, are morals that people share in common.

Moral values are important since they are the one that help us to live in a society. When everyone follows fundamental moral tips, it gives an atmosphere of trust and safety. If it were not for morals, it would be difficult to learn how to behave or what to expect from others.

Why Are Morals Important?

Morals are a familiar and deeply held set of values that we apply to guide our own behavior. We use these values to justify our decisions, to ourselves and others. Morals are more of a psychological construct than ethics. Here are a few reasons why morals matter:

- **Building Trust**: When you live a life of morals, people know that they can trust you. Trust is important in life in all aspects, in friendships, family and even work because when you promise something, others know that you will do it.
- **Creating Harmony**: Morals help us to get along on a daily basis. When we live our lives with

moral values, including honesty, generosity, and justice, we help others in our society to have a good quality of life.

- **Guiding Decisions**: Life is full of tough decisions. Morals are like your compass, that help you to take the right path on your way to the top when you're faced with difficult choices. For example, if you come across a wallet in the street, your morals may lead you to give it back to its owner instead of keeping the money inside.

Common Examples of Morals

While morals can differ from person to person, some are commonly shared across many cultures. Here are a few examples:

- **Honesty**: Truthfulness and being sincere. Honesty is essential because it acts as the glue holding people together. Also, honesty helps a person to conquer problems and excel in life.
- **Respect**: Being respectful is another important thing you can do to make people like you. If people don't respect you, they won't want to be your friend or help you with anything, and no one will like hanging out with you. It's difficult for someone to like a person when they don't respect them.
- **Responsibility**: Being accountable for your actions. Responsibility means doing what you are supposed to do and accepting the consequences—

for example, if you break a toy on purpose, you're responsible for replacing it.

- **Fairness**: Treating all people the same. Fairness means recognizing that our biases exist and taking action to address them so that all people have an opportunity to succeed, regardless of their background or lived experience.
- **Compassion**: Taking care of each other and being kind especially when they are in need, compassion makes us human our ability help the ones who are in suffering or distress.

How Do We Develop Morals?

Morals are not something you are born with, but rather something you gradually nurture over time. In most cases morals are learned from your parents at a young age and as you grow, develop, and move onto high school and college you learn them from society.

- **Family Influence**: The first concepts of morality we know, come from our families. Parents teach their children what behaviors are right and wrong by setting examples and by explaining the appropriate rationales.
- **Education**: Schools also have a big part to play in teaching morals and moral values. Usually, school environments tend to educate students along the lines of what is acceptable behavior and what is not. For instance, students are taught about

the importance of being honest, about showing respect to others, about fair-play in games in which they take part, and so on. My school syllabus had a subject dedicated to Moral Science.

- **Religion and Culture**: Many people are taught morals by their religion or their own cultural traditions. This is important because often these guidelines on how to live a good life as well as what values one should hold, are extremely clear.
- **Personal Experiences**: It is true that as people age, the lessons they learn from personal experience, and the ways in which they behave as a result, can shape their moral principles. People can learn from what actually happens to them and from observing what happens to others. For example, if having lied causes one person to get into trouble and it causes another person to be seen as untrustworthy, then a young child may conclude that lying is bad.

Morals and Financial well-being

You may be thinking, 'what do morals have to do with money?' The truth is – they are actually connected. It takes strong morals to achieve financial well-being — being able to support yourself without depending on anyone else.

Here's how:

In the world of work and business, integrity, honesty and trust are all valuable assets that can open doors and gain you recognition. If you act with integrity and honesty, both personally and professionally, and people know they can trust you to keep your word, you'll likely be given opportunities to do more than your current role demands. But if you're generally dishonest or mistrustful of others, people won't give you additional responsibilities or recognize your abilities.

Equally important is the connection between financial responsibility and financial well-being. This covers budgeting, saving and sensible investment.

Respect is central to valuing and appreciating the work you do and the work of others. Pricing your services unfairly devalues the hard work that you do. Similarly, when you underpay someone else for their work, it devalues them. (the dissatisfaction of being in a corporate job, stems from this)

Morals are what create a good, successful life. They are what keeps us honest, build trust and respect with others, and they help us obtain financial well-being. If we know and live by strong moral principles not only will our personal lives be better but we can reach our financial goals honestly, fairly, and will feel fulfilled in the process.

- Morals are what societies consider right and acceptable.
- Morals are the criteria of behaviour that are shared and they help people in living together in groups.
- Morality of the majority is evident in their following of the social norms.

Exercise:

Write down the 5 moral values that matter most to you (e.g., honesty, responsibility, fairness, respect, compassion)

1.

2.

3.

4.

5.

Reflect on Each Value: For each value, write a few sentences about why it matters to you.

1.

2.

3.

4.

5.

Case Study

Amit's Journey to Financial Well-being and Fulfillment

As a 50-year-old financial analyst, Amit worked hard and smart to build wealth over the years in anticipation of a secure future. Being financially independent did not mean he no longer needed to work. In fact, on the contrary, it gave him freedom to explore things he always wanted to do in life.

Challenge: Amit faced several challenges:

- How to become Financially Independent: He had to make sure that whatever he did, his investments and savings generated enough money to support his family's lifestyle without relying on active income.
- Transitioning into a new dimension: After Amit was self-sufficient financially, he had to move on from the job-based mind set to one that sought fulfillment and passion in what you do.
- Balancing Leisure and Purpose: And then he had to figure out how to use that freedom—how not just to fill his time, but to spend it.

How he did it: Amit's strategy was based on Purposeful Financial Planning and Pursuing Passions. Here are the steps to his success.

Achieving Financial well-being:

- Strategic Savings and Investments: Amit consistently saved and invested during his working years. He concentrated on diversifying his investment portfolio in order to achieve long-term financial security.
- Financial Goals: He set financial goals that were clear and reviewed them regularly. He was not hesitant to make changes to his goals in order stay on course for independence.

Embracing New Freedoms:

- Exploring Passions: Amit didn't want to spend all his time working. He had always wanted to travel the world, paint and learn a musical instrument. Now, he could do all those things!
- Pursuing Hobbies: Amit joined few clubs and communities of his interest. He also felt happy by seeing similar people around and exploring new interests.

Finding Purpose and Joy:

- Volunteering and Giving Back: Amit spent his spare time doing volunteer work and participating in fund raisers for causes he believed in. It helped him give back to the community and feel fulfilled.

- Personal Development: He created a focus to participate in courses and workshops for further learning in areas of interest.

Creating a Balanced Life:

- Mindful Scheduling: In his opinion, he could do justice to his life outside office only if he led a well-balanced and healthy life. Thus, he made sure that no matter what, his hobbies, leisure activities and health did not take a back seat.
- Reflective Practices: He practiced mindfulness and reflection to appreciate how far he has come and stay connected with his core values and goals.

Amit's results to financial well-being led to:

- Fulfillment and Joy: Amit discovered some of his true fulfillment and joy from pursuing passions and hobbies, which also enriched his life beyond the accumulation of money.
- Personal Growth: Pursuing interests and volunteer work continued to be avenues for personal growth and a sense of purpose.
- Inspiration to Others: Amit's story is inspiring. I know several people who have read it and have subsequently starting thinking about their own journey towards financial well-being, and how they can use their resources to pursue their passions or help others.

Amit's story tells us one thing clearly – financial well-being is not just about having money. It's also about the freedom to use your money to do what you really want to make yourself happy and be at peace. And with some good planning, it's possible to do that and still make a difference, a richer and more satisfying difference.

"Success usually comes to those who are too busy to be looking for it." — Henry David Thoreau

Reality Check!

Do any of these circumstances sound like something you've experienced?

- **Debt Worries**: Dealing with debt such as credit cards, loans, or home loans can be stressful. It can create guilt, especially if you value being financially secure.
- **Living vs. Saving**: There are many people who can't decide between living life now and saving their money in case they live too long in retirement. They call this FOMO (Fear of Missing Out), but also want the safety of saving.
- **Generosity vs. Security**: If you like to support others, it may be hard for you to hold back money from family, friends or charitable causes in order to save for your own future.
- **Keeping Up Appearances**: Sometimes, people are forced by the society to lead a life that they cannot afford; by this I am not referring to rich people who want more and more. Here I am referring to people from lower income strata who are falsely encouraged by the society, not to live on less if they can afford more. For example,

buying a bike or car, because other people in your social surroundings have them. In other words: "Why should you save money when you can enjoy it now?"

- **Hard Work and Sacrifice**: Achieving financial success often requires hard work and ambition. Sometimes this means sacrificing time with family or personal well-being.

If any of this sounds familiar, it's because there is a close tie between financial choices and moral principles. Meeting these challenges requires not just being money savvy, but self-knowledge and an ability to integrate your values consistently with your daily life.

Financial freedom is the ultimate freedom. It's the ability to make decisions without being overly stressed about the financial impact, while also having enough resources not to worry if life decides to throw you a googly. But true financial well-being doesn't come from having money. It comes from ensuring that you manage your finances in a way that is congruent with your highest values so that you can have wealth without sacrificing your relationships, well-being or integrity in the process

But what happens if we take this same line of thinking to morality, in general, not just our money?

"The goal isn't more money. The goal is living life on your terms."

— Chris Brogan

The Universal Power of Morals

As defined earlier, Morals are the rules that govern how we conduct ourselves and judge our own behavior as good or bad, right or wrong, responsible or irresponsible. Morals apply to all aspects of life. Morals guide every individual's understanding of what is considered acceptable.

Just as honesty is important in money management – keeping things transparent, avoiding fraud and building trust – honesty is important in personal relationships, professional pursuits or even with yourself. The moral value of Honesty does not get changed whether we are dealing with finance or other areas of life. It simply directs us to lead a life of Integrity and Authenticity.

The Ripple Effect of Financial Morals

The morals you practice in your financial life are not separate from everything else. They radiate outward, informing the rest of your moral code. If you live by values like responsibility, generosity and fairness with money, those values will also take root in other domains. We can see that all the effort put into achieving moral clarity in one arena of life can cause moral growth across the board.

Someone who budgets carefully and avoids debt may find that their sense of responsibility spills over into other important areas of their life, such as taking care of their health, keeping commitments, and fostering healthy relationships. Moral discipline in one area tends to spill over into other areas.

Expanding the Moral Compass

As we transition from morality through the lens of money to morality more broadly, it's important to remember that the very 'money mindset' principles that guide us in daily financial decision-making are actually embedded within a broader set of guiding principles — a moral compass — that governs our dealings with life's many and varied moral challenges. In other words, when we're facing any kind of challenge, be it a financial choice or interpersonal conflict or opportunity to help our community, we use this same set of deeply held values and beliefs to guide our response.

Consider the value of fair dealing. In business, fair dealing might involve not taking advantage of others or not putting your interests ahead of the interests of your employer. Fair dealing in life asks us to treat others with respect, seek justice, and put ourselves on equal footing with others when making decisions. The principle is unchanged; only its application expands.

By recognizing that morals of in the financial domain are also connected with other areas of life, we will be able to realize that the quest for financial well-being is not purely on a financial level but on a moral one. This understanding prompts us to develop an all-encompassing view of morality which spurs us to honour our values in all aspects of life.

So, let us start to know about Morals and how it impacts our lives.

What are Morals shaped by?

This is a question that requires some serious self-reflection. To know what influences our morality, is to really know ourselves and how we interact with the world. Morality isn't made up of imagined theories floating around in space somewhere; they're the 'rules' that govern each of our behaviors, actions, decisions, and interactions with other people; but what factors help form them and lead them to be so variable in all of us?

I got you thinking huh? Anyways, let's see how are morals formed, what shapes them?

The Influence of External Parties

Morality evolves over time, constantly updated by innumerable influences that subtly and collectively work to reshape our most precious mental resource from infancy to adulthood. For better or worse, few of these influences are stronger than the people we encounter outside our own skin, in family, culture, school, religion and peers—the sources of many (most?) of the values that drive how we think and behave.

- The Family: The First Moral Sculptors

  Family is usually the first and often most important moral teacher for an individual. Since infancy, humans are embedded in a familial setting where norms and values are systematically –and sometimes subtly– engrained in the growing person. Parents, or whoever stands as guardian for a child, become this moral instructor who teaches us –formally or not– what is right and what is wrong. By doing and not doing certain things; by saying and not saying others; by choosing to do one thing rather than other, they are building our own little by little but long-lasting moral construct. Justice, empathy, truth, or responsibility starts being experimented when we draw our first breath on our mothers' arms.

For example, if a family prizes honesty above all else, it's more likely that their children will similarly embrace honesty as a supreme value. On the other hand, families who accept or even reward lying in certain situations can instill in their children nuanced attitudes about the importance of speaking the truth. Early moral teachings become etched into our sense of self and remain throughout our lives, continuing to influence how we confront ethical problems and think about justice.

"The family is the first essential cell of human society."

— Pope John XXIII

- Cultural and Social Norms: The Collective Moral Code

  Beyond the immediate family, our morals are shaped by culture and society. Every society has its own customs, rules, and traditions that guide how people should behave. These rules come from places like the government, media, public discussions, literature, and laws.

  Culture is like an experiment that shows us that most of what we learn comes from society. It helps us understand that we can't fully develop as humans without culture and society. Culture explains a lot about why people behave the way they do and what they believe is right or wrong.

  People learn these rules through socialization, which includes education, how they consume media, and being part of different communities. These experiences help people lean towards doing what they believe is morally good.

  However, sometimes culture and society can also promote rules and beliefs that are wrong or harmful, like supporting unfair practices or not recognizing the value of others. When faced with such norms, people might either accept them or question and think critically about them.

  An example is; how collectively we stereotype certain people or groups. It is something that is taught by a group or society and not something we are born with.

- Religion: The Moral Compass of Faith

One of the most powerful external influences on morality has been religion. Everywhere around the world, people's religious beliefs and behaviours have been some of the closest to their hearts and some of the most influential on their judgments. Religious texts and traditions are not just storehouses of virtue; they are supposed to be transcriptions of the word – or words – of God (or gods).

Religious institutions and religious leaders are often perceived to be the bearers of these moral teachings, sometimes as direct divine commandments that one must adhere to in order to attain spiritual well-being or to avert God's wrath. This is also evident through the impact of religion on morality as reflected in the legal, customary and everyday normative behavior of societies, for example, in relation to the moral prohibitions imposed on theft, murder or lying that have found their way into legal systems as seemingly universally agreed upon moral norms.

But the moral sway of religion isn't so massive; different religions — and even different sects within the same religion — can have very different visions of what it means to be good or bad. This is a source of moral and ethical tension within people, within groups and across groups.

In some religion, people do not eat animal meat as it is against their moral while in some other religion, eating meat is totally acceptable.

- Education & Peer Influence: The Shapers of Moral Reasoning

Education is another big factor in how we develop our morals. In school, we learn about different ideas, including many ethical theories and examples from history. Education doesn't necessarily teach us to be better people, but it helps us think more clearly about right and wrong.

Teachers, as authority figures and role models, can greatly influence the moral development of children. The values that teachers promote, like respect, honesty, and fairness, can shape how students view morality. School rules, policies, and the overall atmosphere can also reflect a community's or a country's moral values and affect students' ideas about what is right and wrong.

Peers also play a big role in the moral development of children and teenagers. During the teen years, when friends and social interactions become more important, peer relationships can both support and challenge the moral values learned at home or in other social circles.

Friendships and being part of social groups provide chances to discuss and explore moral beliefs. These experiences can strengthen existing values or lead to adopting new ones.

- The Media: The Modern Moral Storyteller

In the contemporary world, media has become the most powerful tool for us to shape our morality. We are constantly being fed with different types of films, dramas, songs, music videos, internet media, so on and so forth that contain certain messages about what is right or wrong; as well as what we should do or not do to be considered a good person. Pictures of heroes in media show us what heroic acts should be like if we desire to become a true hero. Media representations of justice also imply on us whether it is right or wrong to kill other people for the sake of revenge.

The representation of different types of families in popular TV shows can also undermine the perceived authority of traditional moral views about family structures, and news reports about social justice movements can lead people to feel moral outrage and a motivation for change.

Social media in particular has expanded the impact of external factors over our morals, by facilitating the fact that ideas and values can now so rapidly and massively increase, often generating shifts in public moral sentiment.

However, media's impact on morality definitely has a dark side. Media can promote ideals and values that are in line with positive moral ethics, but media can also expose kids to negative influences that are contradictory to the values on which we're trying to raise them – or even create fearful reactions. With the increasingly diverse forms of media available in today's world, children are constantly given loads of messages that invite them into "moral discourse." In order for this power of the media to be constructive it must be steered towards a very different kind of reflection than that which is offered in many books and articles written about media and morality.

The Relationship of External Forces

The morals we have is a continuous relationship between our internal reflection and the influence of the external. Of course, I would like to say that our moral compass is totally self-directed, but we can't deny that our family, culture, religion, education, peers and media contribute in a huge part in defining what is right or wrong.

It's not like they exist separately but they are influencing each other sometimes mutually reinforcing sometimes creating moral dilemmas.

Knowing how external factors influence our morals allows us to trace the origin of our moral intuitions and – hopefully – gives us a little bit of extra traction when we think about how we might want to revise or refine these conditions. Given that moral values are shifting around us more rapidly than ever, knowing some of the causes of those shifts is surely becoming more important.

Exercise:

Reflect on your surroundings, and list down, who in your life has the most influence in shaping your Morals? List down any incidents or observation that you can remember.

It is possible that different individuals/groups influenced different morals, note them down.

Examples: In my life:

- My father – Mr. Babasaheb Ghag influenced 'Hard-Work' – I used to see my father get up for work early in the morning, travelling via bus, and never missing a day.
- My teacher – Mrs. Meena Vaishampayan influenced 'Kindness' – She used her own money to pay for my computer class, without even me or my parents realizing it.

- My Football coach – Mr. Diego influenced 'Discipline' – He selected players in the team on the basis of discipline first, then skills.

Influencer	**What Moral**	**Incident/Observations**

Moral Dilemmas

Moral dilemmas are situations in which individuals are challenged with contradictory moral principles or difficult choices. These dilemmas test the strength and flexibility of one's moral values, as they require individuals to make decisions that may challenge their established beliefs. But, how do these dilemmas occur?

The Dilemma of Laxman

Laxman was a 28-year-old marketing professional, who lived in Mumbai - a city that never slept. He had slogged and toiled for years to reach where he was then, beginning as a junior marketing associate right after finishing his college; eventually gaining promotions upon promotions – gaining repute in the industry along with it and also being known for his integrity. Life was good, but like most of the youngsters Laxman too had often found himself stuck between aspirations and reality.

One evening, Laxman got a call from his old college mate, Raam. Raam had just joined a multinational corporation that was the talk of the town when it came to everything related to digital marketing. "Laxman there's an opening in our firm and trust me you're the one for it" said Raam all excited. "The pay is fantastic, unbelievable actually and so are the perks. Apart from that you'll have an opportunity to work with some of THE best brains in the industry!"

Laxman was intrigued. He had been in his job long enough and while he liked it, the thought of a new challenge, with a massive raise, interested him. Raam told him about the details and Laxman's eyes opened wide. This could be that proverbial once-in-a-lifetime position. With this job he would be able to pay-off his education loan and save without issues for a home. He would also be able to help his parents who had made so many sacrifices to give him such a great education.

But as Raam went on with the conversation, Laxman felt less and less excited. It was a company known for 'fire to the rain' marketing strategies; some that were even advertised wrongly or unprofessionally. They were all over the news advertising for sensitive groups with false information and sometimes they advertised products that did not meet their expectations. Laxman had always taken pride in his job of being honest, he had never pushed a product he did not believe in nor misrepresented a customer for the sake of profit.

That night Laxman had no peace of mind. His thoughts were like a powerful flood. The job offer was one in a million. It provided as much as prestige, financial security and the right to join the leaders in the business world. But it wasn't for free. Laxman would have to abandon his principles on that way, and that didn't settle with him.

Days became weeks and Laxman still hadn't made a decision. He spoke to his parents. They were over the moon for him. "Beta, this is your chance to make something big of yourself," his father had said. "You've worked so hard and now it'll be time to reap the rewards." His mother was equally as excited. She imagined, as only a mother can with rose-tinted glasses, the day Laxman would buy his own home.

But deep-down Laxman felt uneasy. He couldn't help but feel that he would be selling out if he took the job. He had always maintained that one should do what is right, no matter how hard it is to do it. And when he was being put to the test on the very subject that could determine his future, doubt had started to creep into him.

One evening Laxman went for a walk to sort things in his head. He walked the busy streets of Mumbai until he came to a small temple he used to go to when he was in college. He went inside and sat there silent, finding solace in the quiet.

A page was turned in Laxman's life, and he sat back, focusing on the lessons that his grandparents instilled in him- of always doing what is right. 'You can't have a success that will cost you your morals,' this is one thing his grandfather had told him once. '**You may gain the world, but you will lose yourself**.'

Laxman closed his eyes, taking a deep breath. He had made up his mind. The following day he called Raam and turned down the job offer. Raam sounded surprised and did his best to try and talk him out of it, but Laxman was resolute. "Thanks for the opportunity, Raam, but this just isn't me – I have to be authentic."

After that phone call, Laxman felt better. It wasn't an easy decision to make but it was one that made sense. He knew he'd make less money, but he'd also be genuinely happy. And with a perspective like that, Laxman was ready to prosper where he currently was anyway. He didn't need that new job because he would thrive on his own terms.

Over the next few months, Laxman continued working away and his integrity didn't go unnoticed. His company started giving him more and more responsibilities and eventually he was put in charge of a project that won an award in their industry. His career was taking off, and most importantly, he was glad to have listened to himself and made the decision he had.

Laxman's story is evidence to the fact that as much as we would like to think it is money that defines us, it's actually our values. In a world where we are constantly looking for the easy way out, where do I sign up for? and how can I get away with it? is seen as smart, Laxman's story begs to differ. Success not only depends on where you end up but more importantly the path you take to get there.

Just like Laxman, at some point in our lives we all come across such situations where moral dilemmas keep on eating our personal space.

Let's distinguish the Moral Dilemmas to get clarity.

Characteristics of Moral Dilemmas

Moral dilemmas share certain key features that distinguish them from other kinds of problems of rational choice:

- Conflict of Values: A moral dilemma represents conflict between two or more ethical principles or values. For instance, a person might have to decide between the choice of being truthful and protecting someone's feelings.
- No Clear Resolution: Moral dilemmas are called 'dilemmas' because they pose 'problems' for which there are no cut-and-dried solutions that

can be relied upon. Any decision made will likely compromise some moral principle. Every solution is inherently imperfect in some way.

- Significant Consequences: The options in a moral dilemma are usually not minor, involving potential harm to the welfare of others, compromising the moral integrity, or producing some other kind of serious morally objectionable outcomes in social or institutional context.

Moral Dilemmas can create more emotional and psychological tension as it touches the difficult choices and the possible moral compromises. Notice that individuals may feel guilty, anxious, or harsh as they are wrestling with a dilemma.

Types of Moral Dilemmas

Moral dilemmas can also be classified based on the nature of the moral conflict in question, and/or the structure of the moral conflict itself. Common examples of types of moral conflicts or dilemmas include:

- Personal Dilemmas: These dilemmas occur when a decision needs to be made which would either affect the person directly or people close to him or her. For example, a person may face a dilemma whether to report about his friend's unethical act, wherein he or she knows that reporting such an act can lead to end of their friendship, but at the same time it helps in ensuring justice.

This example of the age-old train problem assumes a situation in which a train is heading towards five people tied to a track. The only way you can save them is to pull the lever and divert the train onto another track where it will kill one person instead. What will you do? This dilemma makes you make a choice whether to actively harm in order to save more lives or to refrain from doing anything that can cause more damage by letting something happen.

- Organizational Dilemmas: In a work place or an organizational set up, people tend to get into dilemma when they have responsibilities towards more than one party or stake holder and it is not feasible for them to be fully loyalist to both due to conflicting interests. For example, an employee whose company policy does not allow him to replace a product which has manufacturing defects however his loyalty towards the company also demands him that he does not cheat the customer either.

An employee finds out that a close co-worker has been engaging in unethical conduct which could potentially cause thousands of dollars of losses for the company. Either the employee can stay loyal to the co-worker and remain silent, or be honest and report the bad behavior, which would result in certain severe consequences for the close co-worker as well as possibly himself.

- Social Dilemmas: These are the type of dilemmas, which involves much more than individual or the group. They involve issues that question whole of society and in which an individual or a group is forced to choose between two or more competing social goods.

  Example of such dilemmas is: A therapist is told by a patient that the patient plans to kill several people. The therapist is faced with a moral dilemma: reporting this to the relevant authorities, and in so doing ensuring that potential victims are protected, involves breaching patient confidentiality, an essential ethical commitment for any therapist.

- Ethical vs Legal Dilemmas: At times a moral dilemma is created in the mind due to the conflict between the requirements of the law and what is ethically right.

  For example, A doctor has five dying patients, each of whom needs a different organ in order to survive. Unfortunately, there are no organs available for any of them, except for one healthy person who could donate his organs. Should the doctor kill that person and distribute his organs to the five dying people in order to save their lives? In doing so, he would be saving five lives at the expense of one life.

Moral dilemmas by their nature are complicated, and sometimes there is no one 'right' solution to the problem. In the process of choosing between different ethical principles it is necessary to take into account the potential consequences of a decision and also to reflect upon one's values and moral beliefs. People may sometimes need to give priority to one moral principle over another which may result into hard compromises.

The trick with moral dilemmas is that 2 people could react to one situation differently and choose two different routes. This is because of their moralities, culture practices and personal way of doing things. The right choice can be different depending on who you are, which causes many arguments over what the real 'right' is.

It is especially indirect to have a conflict of conscience because you are aware that with whatever decision shall come consequences, good or bad. Sometimes two things come in front of you and you have to choose one, that is where you end up being guilty, regretful or in doubt. It is normal because it demonstrates the boundaries of our opportunities, grounded in misleading truths and reveals that we live in an imperfect world.

But it is also important to realise that confronting such harrowing moral dilemmas itself is necessary for ethical maturity. These experiences help us get a handle on our own values, shape up our moralizing thought process and therefore we are able to have more empathy towards others.

Now how many times have you come to a crossroad which make you commit to one choice or the other? This is where you had to make choices between two or more morally justifiable but mutually exclusive options. Many a times, right?

Try to remember 2 – 3 such instances.

When I was about 12 years old, one Saturday evening I was returning home after playing with my friends, and just as I am about to reach my apartment, I see a wad of cash lying on the floor. I picked it up, and thus started my Moral Dilemma.

- Did anyone see me picking it up? – NO
- Who does it belong to? – Don't Know
- Did I need the money? – YES
- Did it belong to me? – NO
- What should I do? – I was conflicted between Honesty and Greed.

At that point, I just ran up the stairs to see if the rightful owner is still on their way, and there I saw an uncle going up the stairs towards his home. I asked him if he dropped some cash, and he was really happy to have received the lost money.

An important life lesson learnt – something happened and tried to overpower my moral of honesty, but in that few seconds of decision making, I could see myself as a dishonest person for the rest of my life if I kept the money. I chose my moral – and till date whenever I am faced with such a dilemma, the choice is easier.

Such moral dilemmas will test you, especially when you are faced with some kind of hardship, be it financial, in a relationship, at work, dealing with government workers, etc. Who comes out on the other side, often decides the kind of life you chose for yourself.

Exercise:

Write down the instances that you can remember, where you were faced with a Moral Dilemma.

- What was the incident?

- What was the dilemma?

- What did you choose?

- Impact of that choice?

Moral Erosion

Have you ever been in a situation and said to yourself, "Whoa I wouldn't have reacted like this last year but why am I acting all different now?" That's when you know you're probably experiencing Moral Erosion.

For example, let's say you used to consider yourself someone who was always truthful, even in those really tough spots. And yet recently, you've found yourself telling a little white lie to either avoid having to deal with something or gain some sort of marginal upper hand. It's something that would have never sat right with you in the past, and now it just comes out.

This subtle shift of your moral compass when slowly through time, your norms and values start to deteriorate and you will start to do the things you didn't use to do.

Moral erosion refers to the undoing or decline of moral values and ethical behavior within an individual or a society. It describes changes in how individuals are guided by their own set of moral values. Such quality and behavioural changes generally take place over an extended period of time and often remain unnoticed because people around us also behave similarly. Moral erosion can also occur due to the influence of external circumstances, such as other people, city life, monotonous routines, lack of positive influences etc.

Moral decline is a gradual deterioration of ethical standards, which becomes more and more apparent with small compromises or minor tolerances. In the beginning, a person is asked to accept something taking place in a certain way, which actually he might not perceive as terrible. He might agree to it when others present will do so. But this process repeatedly helps him became accustomed to big violations for what he would not give his approval at once.

For instance, think about a person in a high position of power who might begin by taking small favors or gifts that don't seem like much. But, as this person continues to get favoured with such perks, he may start to justify more serious and ethically vague transgressions–such as making allowances for violations when it comes to certain rules or conducting themselves wrongly. What started off as a minor carelessness can soon snowball into outright corruption.

Causes of Moral Erosion

Moral values of humans can deteriorate due to various reasons, be it of an individual or of the society. Sometimes the reasons merge and increase the speed of decline.

- One of the biggest reasons for erosion of morals is when one finds a way of justifying his immoral acts. Maybe he may keep telling himself, "It's manageable," "It's not so bad," or "I deserve this." Such are common excuses that might lead an individual to continue downhill in acting unethically.

- Oftentimes moral decline takes place gradually. This is referred to as incrementalism. It's always set into motion by those little actions, which look so trivial, but each little slip becomes the rationalization for the next one. And pretty soon, all these steps add up, and there will be a big moral change that we can't see because it's taken place so slowly.
- The influence of immoral friends is also a cause of moral decline. Being with them, one might start following them even if one knows it is wrong. For instance, one could take the example of a person who calls themselves a friend of a thief and does not report the case of theft just because they do not want their friend to get into trouble, and they may lose their sense of honesty.
- The standards held by society are subject to adjustments; therefore, moral deterioration may be observed. When new ideas and behavior become the vogue, the old rules of morality seem out-of-date. This can also occur in business, where a practice that is considered wrong in the past is today accepted as normal.

- If one was constantly bombarded with the display of corrupt or evil activities by numerous people, then they become used to it and a sensitivity to such activities decreases. Consequently, the standard of morality also decreases. States become more and more prone to corruption, where things that are wrong start to become normal. This can happen in work settings, in businesses, or in nations.

Some people don't think there really are absolute rules about what is right and wrong. If they believe that moral rules are just social guidelines and they don't work in every situation, then they adjust their behavior according to the situation. This may result in unethical actions, for they would think that rules can be bent as the situation demands.

The Consequences of Moral Erosion

Moral decline has adverse effects on individuals as well as the society. As moral values erode in any situation, relationships, institutions, and systems that depend on these values gradually crumble away.

- Loss of Trust: Of all the immediate repercussions of moral debasement, one that stands out most is the loss of trust. When individuals or organizations participate in unethical practices, they undermine the trust that others put in them. This can result in unhealthy relationships, loss of credibility and even social disintegration.

- Corruption: When moral values are compromised, which commonly happens in the absence of ethical standards, choice of corruption becomes more common. Corruption involves the exchange of goods, services, or privileges in return for something prohibited. In a corrupt society, inequality and injustice may also prevail, and democratic institutions suffer erosion.

- Dehumanization: With the decrease in moral standards, it presents danger in regarding others as not human being but just mere tools to an end it can cause the following problems exploitation, discrimination and violence.

- Erosion of Social Norms: Moral erosion if not checked timely, results in the erosion of social norms and social values. It creates an atmosphere or a culture of cynicism where everybody begins to lack trust and have no faith in the workability of any ethical systems and standard. That is, being unethical becomes the normal behavioural practice.

- Psychological and Emotional Impact: At the individual level, moral erosion may create a wide range of psychological and emotional problem. As people turn their backs on their values they can feel guilt, shame, and a blow to self-respect. Eventually, this might take you down to anxiety, depression, as well as moral disorientation.

Preventing and Addressing Moral Erosion

Given the grim costs of moral decline, we need to make prevention of such decline a high priority – socially and individually.

- Self-Awareness and Reflection: Human beings can fight against moral decline by being aware of their self and reflecting about their values and behaviour. They shouldn't lie to themselves, they should never bet on the justification, they should admit small corruptions, and they always are to remain careful about what they really are doing.
- Ethical Leadership: it is possible for organization and societies to prevent the moral erosion by spreading ethical leadership. Leaders who demonstrate ethical conduct, hold themselves and others responsible for the same, and create a culture of integrity can help stop the slow degeneration of moral principles.
- Education and Training: Educating and training on ethics can be a way to help individuals learn the values with which they can approach ethical dilemmas, and acquire the skills required to deal with those challenges. This involves the teaching of critical thinking, ethical decision making as well as the importance of integrity.
- Accountability and Transparency: Implementation of accountability and transparency can avoid

moral degeneration. When it is difficult for corruption to breed due to the fact that individuals and organizations are responsible for their performances and their mandates, and the returns on corrupt practices can be easily monitored, these negative acts will be reduced.

Preventing moral decay can be done by societies through enhancing the social norms and values morally. This can be manifested through public education, community mobilisation and promotion of morality in all spheres of life.

Moral courage, the readiness to speak out against wrongdoing even when it involves risk, is an indispensable antidote to moral decline. If people come forward and act honestly and courageously even in difficult situations, ethical standards are more likely to be maintained.

Moral decay is a slow and gradual process that eventually leads to the weakening of the moral fibre of a society, organization or an individual. If it is not checked timely than it keeps on progressing for worst leading to the ills like lack of trust, cheating, scam, corruption and increased crime rate in the society thereby making conditions worse day by day.

The starting point to prevent moral decline is to understand its causes and effects. By developing self-awareness, encouraging moral leadership and normalizing positive behaviors in society, we can prevent standards from slipping and ensure that such values continue to underpin a just, fair and prosperous society.

Why did we speak about Moral Erosion? Because this aspect needs to be immediately identified within ourselves. If there has been a decay in morals, it might be restraining your journey of financial well-being.

Exercise:

Identify and list down any morals you previously lived by, and don't use them anymore.

1.

2.

3.

4.

5.

The Role of Morals in Society

Morals are the unshakable bonds that hold together the community, which in turn makes civilization possible. They are the sturdy beams upon which human society has been erected throughout history. They also serve as our committed assistance in distinguishing between the right and wrong path in life. Morals are one of those things we refuse to live without. In short, we must think of how serious a matter it is when people let its grasp on the meaning of 'morals' become vague.

Morals as the Foundation of Trust

At the core of all relationships—whether among individuals, communities, or nations—is trust. Trust is the expectation that others' future actions will be beneficial to us. It functions as a kind of social principal —an asset that is both valuable to possess and generates benefits when invested in. Trust between buyers and sellers, for instance, lowers transaction costs and enables the marketplace to work more smoothly. A student who trusts a teacher orients their behavior differently than does a student who distrusts her. A citizen who trusts his government obeys the law voluntarily, whereas a citizen who distrusts his government expects that it will behave coercively, and therefore focuses on avoiding the long arm of the law.

In business, ethical values such as honesty and integrity are an important element of creating trust. When organisations and individuals are transparent, keep promises and act fairly in all practice areas, they create the basis on which to develop relationships of trust with customers, business partners and employees. Such trust is not a 'nice to have' – it is essential for sustained success. If, on the other hand, that trust is shaken by a breach of morality, disagreement and conflict emerge.

Morals as a Guide for Justice

Morals are a key factor in the determination of justice. Most laws and legal norms symbolize moral notions, reflecting usual ideas on just and fair treatment. These concepts serve as the necessary guideposts ensuring fairness in the delivery of justice, protection of rights, and rectification of wrongs.

For example, let 's consider the moral principal that all people are equal and deserve equal treatment under the law. This belief has been the building block of civil rights movements all over the world. When society values this moral principle, it becomes more equal and fairer. When this value is neglected or violated, it results to discrimination.

Morals as the Basis for Social Cohesion

A society's moral values define what it means to be a part of that society. Through shared morals, people associate together on the basis of similar culture and beliefs, giving them a common purpose and understanding. They feel as if they are a part of something greater than themselves.

In many cultures, moral values such as respect for the elderly, helping strangers, and taking the welfare of other members in a community seriously are constructed in such a way that they generate social norm and behavior. As long as these moral values are respected by people who share common connection of a particular cultural group or community; with positive attitude toward existence of others, this kind of society has the tendency to progress because there will be strong social bond which allows every single society member to feel responsible for one another.

Morals as a Force for Change

Throughout history, social advancement oftentimes was made by those with moral convictions. When individuals or communities saw something as unjust, and thus immoral, they had the courage to speak out against it. They risked their reputations, their livelihoods, and at times even their own lives.

The fight for freedom, the fight for abolishing sati, the fight for environmental protection; all these revolutions are a result of being morally convinced about something and then taking a stand. In all these cases, people were sure that certain things were just not right. They needed to change and thus they acted upon it. It is this conviction that makes history and will keep on making our Earth a better place to live.

The Future of Morals in Society

As we ponder over what the future has in store for us, it's certain that the importance of morals is not going to decrease. If anything, in this ever more complex and interdependent world of ours, they are probably only going to increase in importance. Be it tackling global issues like climate change, grappling with the ethical challenges of new forms of technological progress or building inclusive and just societies – morals will continue to be our anchor.

The fact that morals can be legitimately debated is exemplified in the debate around one of the newest things to have moral implications – artificial intelligence (AI) and its associated technology. It is clear that the more AI progresses, the more we will be confronted with issues of privacy, autonomy and human dignity, as well as questions about jobs. Decisions taken now based on our morals will determine what AI becomes in future.

The Stable Importance of Morals

In the end, morals are the foundation of society. They shape our lives and our most urgent social issues.

They reinforce trust. They demand justice. They foster loyalty and care. Morals are also how we, as a society or as an individual, decide whether we are comfortable with a certain kind of progress. And so, we're obliged to confront questions that sit at the intersection of morality and progress, just as previous generations did. If we want to build a world where fewer people say technology is ruining their lives — or occasionally even dying for it — then we have some work to do in imagining and creating a future that's truly inclusive and fair. Let us keep grappling with these profound questions of what human values should guide our progress — as individuals, but more importantly as a society where all people can live beautiful, meaningful lives.

'Log Kya Kahenge'

What will people say? – Haven't each one of us, heard this in some form or the other?"

People here imply Society. Why? As morals plays a crucial role in society. It is the very foundation on which laws are formulated, principles of integrity, discipline and the basic etiquettes of how to live are laid, as these aspects influence our sense of belonging and identity to the world around us.

Let's get beyond the fluff, and into the deep and vital parts of life. At every important stage of life, our choices are judged by the moral structures we consciously or unconsciously hold. When we strip away all of society's façades and look at these stages, we see how morals form the architecture of our lives.

Morals affect not just what we do but also who we are. Seeing this helps us to make better decisions based on high-level values when faced with complex and difficult challenges.

Judge

Each and every action of yours is being judged within the perimeters of morals. We are cast in a web of social norms as soon as we are born. Be it as small as how we lift our finger or be it as big as global issues, everything that you'd do will be weighed under morals. Not only by others but by yourself too.

Let's say you have to decide whether to take a well-paying job, but the company offering the job has been said to engage in unethical business practices. You ponder the decision against your own view of what is decent. You may wonder: Should I really work for a company that might wreak havoc on the planet or mistreat its employees, no matter how good it is for my bank account?

This first step of internal judgement is where morality begins.

Influence

Your actions then are influenced positively or negatively.

Once you make a judgement, it begins to act as a sort of moral compass for your decisions and behaviour. It can lead you in a direction that is consistent with what you value. Or the judgement that forms the new belief can pull you in quite a different direction if the wider world puts pressure on your or if there are other judgements and beliefs already rattling around inside you.

Returning to the job offer example, let's say you consult with friends or family. Some friends may urge you to take the job because of the financial security it would afford. Other friends may counsel you against taking the job because of the lack of ethical alignment.

That external input affects how you decide—maybe you're drawn to take the job because you need the money, even though it goes against a personal rule that you should work for a responsible company.

Impact

Finally, you are impacted by that influence and opt to act differently that what you were set to do. The influence that others—and your internal moral compass—exert on your decisions ultimately impacts the choices you make. This impact can manifest as peace of mind and fulfillment when your actions align with your morals or as discomfort and regret when they do not.

Post considering the judgement and what others think, you might refuse the job offer because you need to live by your morals, even if that means not having financial security. Conversely, you might accept the job offer based on the rationale that financial stability is what is most important in your life right now.

The decision you make will affect your future behavior and your own sense of yourself. For example, if you accept the job, you may be tempted to start justifying other compromises in your mind on the grounds that they too are small. Over time, this tendency could snowball until it imperceptibly undercut your moral standards more generally. If instead you refuse the offer on principle, you are likely to increase your commitment to acting morally in the future and under trying circumstances.

Exercise:

List down 3 – 4 instances where you were interrupted from doing something with the statement – "Log Kya Kahenge? (What will people say?)"

For each of these instances, list down:

- What were you about to do (action)

- Who stopped/interrupted you (influencer)

- What did you do next (impact)

Morals and Well-Being

In this chapter, we will glance through the impact of Morals on our well-being. Remember, a healthy mind is needed to achieve what you consider unachievable, hence the importance of relationships, happiness and emotional health is discussed here. This chapter in itself can act as a guiding light for a well-deserved life (as a whole) and not just financial well-being. Read on!

Morals and well-being are inter-connected, providing the basis for a rewarding and purposeful existence. While well-being is commonly understood in terms of good health, financial security, and satisfying relationships, moral integrity is an equally integral constituent of overall well-being. Morals direct us through life, enabling us to live in accordance with our deeply held convictions and facilitating a sense of harmony, psychological equilibrium, and tranquillity.

Morals and Inner Peace

Inner peace is a state of mental and emotional calmness, with no anxious thoughts, fears or worries. It is a state of tranquility and contentment that allows one to live undisturbed by mental stress, anxieties or worries. Everyone treasures the experience of inner peace yet few seem to find it. It is elusive because though we desire it to be our default state of mind when facing the challenges of life, we do not understand how to achieve inner peace nor how to maintain it in the face of life's daily pressures and demands. One factor that influences inner peace more than any other is the degree to which our actions are in line with our moral values and beliefs. This connection between morals and inner peace can perhaps best be understood through the realization that when one lives a life consistent with their highest values and noblest beliefs, they inherently create a world that is beautiful. In essence, living according to your morality creates a practical vision of human life that matches your ideals.

Alignment of Actions with Moral Values

At the heart of peace of mind is living in harmony with our moral code. When what we do reflects what we believe, then we feel whole and complete. The more our actions mirror our beliefs and convictions, the less conflict or turmoil can exist within us, and we become more stable and at peace.

Example: Take, for instance, an individual who values honesty as an elemental moral virtue. By interacting honestly in their day-to-day affairs such as in personal friendships or relationships, at their workplace, and in financial transactions this person feels a sense of agreement with the moral beliefs they have chosen to live by. It is because of this internal coherence of acting in accordance with their values that they are able to experience high levels of self-appreciation and peace within themselves. Conversely, if they were to act dishonestly-lying or deceiving-there would be an absurdity between what they believe and how they behave which gives rise to feelings of guilt, shame or uneasiness thus undermining tranquillity.

Reduction of Internal Conflict

Internal conflict occurs when we have two different opposing ideas that constantly fight for dominance in our minds. It usually causes great distress, and we are unsure of what would be the best decision to take. There are a lot of causes for internal conflicts, but one main cause is when your actions do not align with your values. When there is mis-alignment between our actions and values, it would lead to internal conflicts. This will also cause you to experience a lot of emotional stress as you feel like you're not being genuine and real. You will feel like you're living a lie and covering behind someone else's life. For example, if you believe in honesty but have been lying most of the time, then your action is not aligned with that value which would lead to guilt and internal conflicts.

Imagine someone who cares about being fair or just, and yet is tempted to take unfair advantage of someone whenever doing so is easy and unlikely to be detected. If that person succumbs to such a temptation, then given that he also has some self-awareness, he is likely to feel guilty or ashamed of himself later on for having acted as he did. His own action provides him with evidence that he does not really care after all about being fair or just – or at any rate that he values other things more highly than being fair or just (for example, gaining personal advantages), so that in the event these other things come into conflict with treating people fairly, then he will set aside – and despise himself in so doing – the commitment to fairness or justice he thought he was acting on. By the same token if he acts as his moral convictions tell him, even if doing so is costly or painful for him in one way or another – then this will equip him instead with evidence that his promises are indeed genuine.

The Role of Forgiveness in Achieving Inner Peace

Forgiveness is a moral value that tends to be in short supply within the individual human heart when it comes to relating ourselves or others. Inner peace cannot coexist with continual anger and resentment toward people in our lives, such as family or work associates, nor can it succeed when we are unable to forgive ourselves for mistakes we have made. By practicing forgiveness, we cleanse emotions such as anger and guilt from our hearts and make room for calmness and contentment.

Suppose someone is wronged by a close, trusted friend. If that person holds on to the resentment and relives it over and over, he will not find peace. But if he decides to forgive, he lets go of those negative feelings and instead forgives his friend for the harm done. The forgiveness is based on his conviction in some more general moral principle(s); for example, this might be that nobody is perfect or everybody makes mistakes at some time. In this way, forgiving frees him of that particular source of anger and the resentment that comes with it.

Building Flexibility Through Moral Integrity

Moral integrity, in the face of any challenge life throws at us, comes from our innate moral compass that guides us through life. When we face tough choices and tough times our moral attribute anchors us so we don't compromise with our own self.

In a difficult situation, like being fired from a job, for example, someone with high moral integrity would likely direct their energy toward looking for another job that suited their own ethical principles rather than toward feeling sorry for themselves or using underhanded tactics. This reliance on an internal sense of right and wrong allows them to feel peaceful in tough times because they know that they are doing what they think is right.

The Long-Term Impact of Moral Living on Inner Peace

Short term rewards might motivate us to abandon our principles, but the long-term benefits of living in harmony with our values are profound. Repeatedly acting in ways that contradict our morals eventually eats away at our self-respect, self-trust, and self-contentment. And without these qualities it's impossible to have peace of mind when dealing with the unavoidable complications of life.

Over a lifetime, a person of integrity builds an inner reservoir of self-worth and self-respect. This, in turn, breeds a sense of tranquility and contentment. When we live with integrity, we feel whole because our actions reflect the values printed on our moral compass. We have few regrets — even after roadmaps gone awry — because we know we made decisions with the best information available to us at the time.

Morals as a Guide to Healthy Relationships

Relationships are part of the human experience, we all have them but we certainly don't come with a manual on how to relate. Our relationships with romantic partners, family members, friends and colleagues can have a profound impact on our overall levels of happiness in life.

At the heart of all of these relationships is morality.

Morality refers to our own sense of what is good or bad, right or wrong, and dictates how we behave as partners. It influences who we choose to be in a relationship with and how that relationship develops over time.

The Role of Trust and Honesty in Relationships

Trust is the bedrock of a healthy relationship. And honesty is one of the building blocks of trust. When we're true to who we are in our relationships, it fosters a level of closeness that can only be matched by the deep sense of peace and ease we feel within ourselves when we express the truth.

In a romantic relationship, that could mean being open about your feelings, thoughts, and intentions. If one partner is willing to tell the truth even when it's hard, they're showing that they care more about the relationship's health than their own ego or self-interest. This helps to build trust between partners and allows them to feel safe with each other. On the other hand, repeated dishonesty — no matter how small — erodes trust.

When mistrust creeps into a relationship, insecurity soon follows — which is usually the beginning of the end.

Respect as a Fundamental Moral Value

Respect is also an important moral value that children learn in the family. Families that are too permissive with their children seem to have children that feel they can do whatever they want. It's okay if parents are divorced, or one member of your family has died, as long as you show how much you still care for other members of your family. I believe that my family is not only my parents, but all people whom I dearly love and will never stop.

In a work context, you might demonstrate respect by truly considering someone else's opinion and point of view, even if they are radically different or diametrically opposed to your own. Doing so in a way that makes the other person feel valued and heard can promote a greater sense of collaboration and goodwill.

Disrespect, however, can breed conflict, that can destroy relationships altogether.

Compassion and Empathy in Relationships

Compassion and empathy are both qualities associated with being human. They are not simply about feeling sorry for another person or being able to understand what they might be going through. Rather, compassion refers to the same ability to connect with others on an emotional level and provide personal support, but where we feel joy rather than sadness in their good fortune. In other words, we genuinely love the other person and wish them all the best.

In a friendship, empathy might mean sympathizing with a friend who is going through a tough time, listening when they need an ear, or being compassionate. You may show compassion in your friendship by doing little things to make your friend's day a bit brighter or sharing in their happiness when good things happen to them. Being a good friend and being loyal are other ways of showing empathy and compassion.

Accountability and Responsibility in Relationships

Being responsible for our own actions and then having the courage to be accountable for the mistakes we make is a moral value that should be common to everyone, yet so often this simply is not the case. When you are accountable you are effectively admitting to yourself and others that yes, you have some share in whatever issue or conflict has arisen, and now you will do everything within your power to make things right because your relationship with the other person genuinely matters.

In a family dynamic, if a parent gets mad and says something mean to their child, being accountable would be to say you are sorry for the burst of anger and be open about ways you will try to deal with stress better in the future. This accountability repairs any damage done, but it also shows your child that they too should hold themselves accountable.

Fairness and Equality in Relationships

Fairness and equality are moral values that give relationship balance and protection from being taken advantage of. In a healthy relationship, both partners believe that their needs matter equally, regardless of what they provide to the relationship. It helps to make decisions together and work out problems in a reasonable manner. It discourages imbalances of power, fosters a safe climate for expression and negotiation and promotes the cultural value of respect between equals.

In a relationship, fairness means each person taking on equal parts of responsibilities so it doesn't become one person's job. If one person has to work late, the other would pitch in chores for that day because they would know when their partner has to work late, they'll take over that responsibility. This makes you feel like a team and you don't start resenting your partner.

The Impact of Moral Integrity on Relationships

Moral integrity enhances relationships through reliability and trust. When we practice what we preach (our moral values), others can count on us to be consistent. Being consistent means being predictable which, in turn, creates a safe and secure environment for relationships to thrive.

In a lifelong friendship, moral integrity is being there for your friend when times are good, as well as bad. Being there with support and loyalty over the passage of years creates a bond that will not be broken. Both friends know they can turn to each other during any stage of life if need be.

Morals as a Source of Inner Strength

In hardships individuals usually find inner strength in their values. These values play a role of an anchor stabilizing the person and helping to concentrate on what is important even in the most difficult situations. Morals give a feeling of having a purpose, and it provides essential direction which resilience needs.

Consider a person who says that the most important thing to him or her is being honest. If they are put into a difficult position, for example, if someone at their place of work insists repeatedly that they do something that is dishonest, this person may feel quite a lot of pressure. They might even feel very strained doing what they feel they must do: saying no and then dealing with the aftermath. But in the end, their action speaks louder than words. It is also that very commitment to honesty, which makes them strong enough to deal with such a situation without compromising their own values.

One of the most important building blocks of resilience is, indeed, the capacity to find meaning in hardship. Values are how we make sense of difficult circumstances and how we can view them as opportunities for growth and learning rather than stress or sources of discouragement.

A compassionate person may see a personal tragedy as an opportunity to grow in their ability to be there for others during similar times of loss. Rather than shutting themselves down and wallowing in sadness, they allow their feelings to fuel their actions, and in doing so find immense purpose. This not only prevents them from being destroyed by their own grief but strengthens their resilience by solidifying the importance of their principles.

Morals as a Guide to Ethical Decision-Making in Tough Times

Making ethical decisions can feel particularly challenging when we are facing a crisis. Stress, fatigue, and other factors can make it tempting to compromise on our principles or to look for short-term gains. However, people with strong principles are more likely to act in ways that are consistent with their values even in difficult situations. This kind of ethical decision-making helps build resilience because it means that our actions will be in alignment with our own sense of what is right, reducing any need we might feel afterward for self-justification or regret.

Imagine if you will a business owner who finds themselves in financial trouble and is sorely tempted to cut corners, or even to engage in less than moral business practices to keep that ship floating. But again, their sense of fairness, and their commitment to transparency will simply not allow them to violate those principles. Yes, going the ethical route may make things more difficult at first but it ultimately allows them to maintain an integrity and trust profile that right out of the gate puts them on solid footing for long-term success.

It takes years to build a reputation of integrity, it takes a single crisis to lose it. If you have made honesty, fairness and compassion a part of your life and work from the beginning, it will not only help you navigate your personal crises better, but also attract people and opportunities in your life that help you deal with the crisis. And each crisis then will make you more resilient, because every new crisis is dealt by the values that has been built over many years."

Morals are integral to resilience and coping because they give us a foundation for ethical decision making, decrease inner fighting, and increase the quality of our relationships. Morals also provide a well of strength within us and help us make sense of suffering so we can rebound from defeats. Over time, being loyal to moral values helps us build resilience overall so we can deal with life's difficulties with greater integrity, purpose, and composure. The more we live according to our morals, the more effective we are at bouncing back from failure —and the more resilient we will be in facing life's inevitable hardships.

The Pursuit of Happiness

The pursuit of happiness is a common goal in life, but it is often elusive and can sometimes be equated with a moral reward. Yet while happiness can indeed be short-lived, true and lasting happiness is generally associated with our willingness to live a life that is consistent with our values and principles. In this part we explore the relationship between morality and happiness by investigating three central themes:

1. defining the nature of happiness through the lens of morality
2. negotiating the moral dilemmas which arise on the path to a happy life
3. recognising that moral integrity serves as the foundation for enduring happiness.

Happiness is often defined as a state of well-being that includes both, feelings ranging from satisfaction to intense joy, and a life that reflects one's deepest values and commitments. If we view happiness through the lens of morality, we will need to ask a different set of questions about what sort of life one should lead and what creates a truly happy or flourishing life.

From a moral standpoint, happiness is not merely a particular form of feeling, or a particular condition in which we feel satisfied. Happiness, in the moral sense, is within typical ways of living or forms of activity that are characteristic of human beings at their best.

Example: Let's take a person who considers honesty and integrity as the most important traits in people. Such a person may realize that his happiness largely depends on how truthfully, he expresses those values in his everyday life. If one has the ability to observe the virtue of honesty in their relationships, work and personal interactions they will likely experience a more profound, longer lasting form of happiness which is based on their moral principles.

- Happiness and Purpose: Morality is important for our personal lives, too. The happiness that comes from taking up the moral point of view can be supremely rewarding. For many people, the way to lead a fulfilling life is by having a project in life, or serving some greater good that is larger than themselves in which they believe. This is not a matter of seeking out pleasant feelings or 'positive psychology'; it is about something deeper and richer than that – namely finding a role or purpose in life that you can devote yourself to wholly, and that will therefore bring you a sense of deep satisfaction.

  A teacher who has the zeal to educate the budding minds is likely to feel a sense of happiness that is beyond external rewards. They find happiness in what they are doing as it is connected with their moral responsibility of being instrumental in the well-being and progress of others.

  The pursuit of happiness can be a winding road, as you come up against moral dilemmas.

The better you become at understanding and resolving moral dilemmas, the happier and more fulfilling your life will become.

- The Dilemma Stemming from the Pursuit of Personal Happiness: Among the moral dilemmas that are faced in the quest for happiness, one is the parallel between self-interest and ethical obligations. The difficulty consists in matching an individual's quest for his/her personal happiness with a requirement to act ethically.

  Example: Consider someone who could get ahead in their career by taking credit for a colleague's work. The option that would lead to career advancement may make the person happy in the short term, but it violates their moral value of honesty. If they put their own happiness first and disregard their moral values, they'll likely feel guilty and conflicted, which isn't good for their overall well-being.

- Short-Term Gains vs. Long-Term Well-Being: Another moral dilemma that people face in their lives is the choice between short-term pleasures like fame, power, wealth etc and long-term happiness. Most often than not people are lured by immediate rewards and gains even if it means going against their long-term goals or morals but this only leads to regret and unhappiness later in life.

We can think of a person who enjoys the instant gratification of luxury purchases but also becomes stressed and unhappy from the mounting debt. In this case, the typical consumer's happiness both is and isn't deceptive. If they were to go on purchasing luxury goods at the same rate, then eventually their financial stability would be gone. So, while it seems that their happiness relies on an illusion, it isn't true that they could gain long-term happiness by abandoning that illusion.

- Happiness at the Expense of Others: A major moral dilemma crops up in a situation wherein, for one person's happiness, you'll have to hurt or cause sadness to some other person/people. The ethical question that arises is – Is it okay to be happy if in so doing you are causing pain or injustice to others?

A business owner could make lots of money and be very happy while not treating their employees right. But they would know that their happiness was at the expense of others, so wouldn't that make them feel bad about themselves? Is happiness really happiness if you get it by doing something wrong?

As difficult as they can be to face, the most reliable path to long-lasting happiness is practicing moral integrity, or consistently acting in ways that line up with your ethical principles–even when it's hard. Moral integrity is living in authentic alignment with your deepest values, which translates into a more profound and enduring kind of happiness.

- The Power of Consistency: Moral integrity is based on the premise of consistency - behaving and living in accordance with one's values regardless of the circumstances. Through consistency, one builds up self-respect, trust and inner peace which are all foundations to sustainable happiness.

  Someone who practices kindness all the time, even when they don't feel like it, will probably have a feeling of inner peace and contentment that, those who practice selfish behavior will never know. By being ethical we cultivate this in ourselves and others, which leads to a good life.

- Authenticity and Self-Respect: Moral integrity is entwined with a sense of authenticity—or living in harmony with one's own values. When we behave in ways that are consistent with our deepest values, we experience a congruence between what we think, say, and do—and this strengthens our self-respect. And self-respect is a vital ingredient for happiness that's meant to last.

  Someone who truly values the environment and lives sustainably even if it means personal loss will be happy. It is because he is being himself and he takes pride in it.

In the event of adversity, moral integrity also serves as a cushion that withstands even the hardest blow. If people encounter difficulties, their loyalty to the moral values can aid them in dealing with troubles without detracting from their happiness. This quality is based on a knowledge that they are leading a truthful life which contributes to a feeling of stability and inner peace system.

During a financial crisis, a person who values honesty and refuses to engage in unethical practices, even under pressure, may face some immediate difficulties. But their sense of inner peace and strength will be an enduring source of happiness because they have not compromised their principles - in good times or bad.

The pursuit of happiness is one of the most important driving forces in our lives. It's what gets us out of bed in the morning and motivates us to conquer new challenges. We can only achieve this deep and fulfilling sense of contentment through moral living. Living a life of integrity is about making choices based on your personal beliefs and values. It means choosing to do the right thing in difficult situations, even when nobody else is watching. It also means cultivating a willingness to be accountable for your actions and to depend on an ethical compass when making decisions. Without integrity, we are left with a sense of unhappiness and dissatisfaction that plagues our thoughts and distorts our perception of reality. Most importantly, when we lack integrity, we lose sight of our internal locus of control which robs us of the freedom necessary for true happiness. Ultimately, it takes courage to maintain a strong sense of integrity in today's world. More often than not, doing right by others demands personal sacrifice or may place you in harm's way but choosing not to build your happiness upon the foundation compromises will reward you tenfold in inner peace and self-respect.

The Impact of Moral Conflicts on Emotional Health

Moral conflicts, cases in which our effective behavior run against our own moral convictions, weakens our emotional health. Such conflicts typically involve extreme forms of guilt, shame, and related self-harming emotions and can trigger profound self-hatred and self-contempt.

- Guilt and Shame: This is the big one. When we behave in ways that go against our moral values, we tend to feel guilt and shame as a result. Guilt is an emotional warning sign that most of us learn through socialization. It's the uncomfortable feeling we get in our gut or heart when we have done something wrong or behaved badly. Shame is similar to guilt but differs in that it has a focus on self. It's a painful feeling directed toward how we perceive ourselves becoming a belief system about who we are–that we are somehow bad, wrong, not good enough, or not lovable.

Imagine a person who cherishes honesty. When they lie – perhaps to keep something private, or to protect themselves from the implications of a hard truth – the blame they direct at themselves can be more agonising than anything they might fear from others. It's not only that, they have done something wrong or self-destructive. In violating their own standard, their actions suggest that either their professed ideals were hypocritical all along, or that some part of them – at least on this occasion – simply does not care about acting in line with them. Both reflections are unbearable. The discrepancy between how things are and how they believe things ought to stimulate nervous efforts to bring those two things back into alignment, whether by bending reality to conform with their view of what it should be, or by retreating from their principles.

- Cognitive Conflict: Moral dilemmas cause cognitive conflict, a psychological state in which our behaviours and beliefs start to misalign. Our mind starts registering discomfort and emotional unrest as we find it difficult to reconcile between what we do and what we promote. The longer it remains unresolved, the heavier is the emotional burden.

A person who believes in fairness, but behaves in a way that is biased to benefit themselves rather than others, might experience cognitive conflict —a state of internal conflict that can manifest as stress, anxiety, or general discomfort and that can lead to overall diminished emotional well-being.

- Fear of Judgment: Moral conflicts can bring about Fear of Judgment from others, which intensifies the negative emotions you have. When we Fear that others would judge us because of what we've done, we might withdraw ourselves, isolate ourselves, or become defensive; things that are guaranteed to negatively affect our emotional health.

Someone who betrays a friend may be driven to do so because they fear the judgement of those around them. This could cause them to feel isolated or lonely, and constantly anxious about what the people in their lives think of them since they're worried about whether or not their actions will have any negative effect on how others see them.

The Role of Forgiveness in Emotional Healing

Forgiveness is a powerful tool in our emotional healing. In cases of moral conflicts, asking for or giving forgiveness both helps us to get rid of the emotional pain and to regain the tranquility and equilibrium in our mind.

- Forgiving others: This is restoring emotional balance by 'letting go'- an emotional state will change from a negative one to a positive one, even if the past affair remains unresolved. The impact of anger, resentment, and bitterness can cause havoc on our mental health and general well-being. With the privilege of forgiveness comes liberation from these emotions, so that one may know peace and psychological equilibrium.

  Someone is harmed by a close friend. The person may initially feel angry and hurt. If the person lingers with these negative feelings, however, he or she will likely experience emotional turmoil for a much longer duration than would otherwise be the case. But if this person chooses to forgive his or her close friend, he or she can let go of those negative emotions and begin the healing process, thereby returning again quickly to an emotional state of well-being.

- Self-Forgiveness: Equally important is our ability to forgive ourselves for actions that are in conflict with our moral values. It is important to forgive ourselves because when we hold onto guilt and shame, we cannot learn from the mistakes that we made, and move forward with a renewed commitment to our values. This process is essential for emotional healing and for maintaining our emotional well-being, long-term.

A person that makes an unwise financial choice that is in direct conflict with their deeply held values of maintaining responsibility, might likely experience a great deal of guilt and self-blame. By practicing self-forgiveness, they can admit the mistake, learn a lesson from it and then move on to make wiser choices. This act of self-compassion will restore emotional equilibrium and prevent prolonged emotional distress.

- Restoration of Relationships: Forgiveness, whether it be for someone else or our-self, is also key to restoring and building our relationships back. When we have moral conflicts that have broken a relationship bond with another person or people, forgiveness restores that, allowing the love to flow.

  In a marriage, one partner might feel betrayed by the actions of the other. In such a situation, forgiveness can be seen as the first step towards healing the relationship and restoring emotional intimacy. When a moral transgression occurs, and forgiveness is contemplated, both partners are likely to be motivated to repair the emotional bond so as to develop an even deeper connection.

The relationship between morality and emotional well-being is rich, powerful, and bidirectional. Morality helps secure emotional well-being by contributing to overall consistency and stability in our emotional lives, by guiding us in navigating the emotional pitfalls that arise in the context of moral conflict, and by helping us repair our emotional lives when they have been damaged by offering a path to healing through forgiveness. Understanding the place of morality in our emotional lives can also help protect us against certain forms of manipulation as we work to better navigate intercultural interactions in an increasingly globalized world (Bloom 2017), and it can lead to greater self-knowledge, inner peace, resilience, and well-being (Graham 2018).

Case Study

Vidya's Journey to Debt Freedom through Emotional Well-Being and Morality Vidya, 28, graduated with a business school debt of over six figures. Although she worked at a good job, the weight of her debt was suffocating, and the high-interest rates combined with her increasing cost of living seemed insurmountable. She realized that she needed to address her finances not just from a financial standpoint, but also from a moral/emotional perspective.

Vidya had two main challenges which affected her morale as well as emotional being:

- High-interest student loans that seemed insurmountable.
- Limited income prevented her from an extra payment and she felt trapped and worried.

Solution: Vidya approached her financial challenges with a focus on emotional well-being and a strong sense of morality.

Here's how she navigated her journey to debt freedom:

Debt Consolidation with Mindful Decision-Making:

- Research and Moral Reflection: Vidya didn't just research various debt consolidation options, she also spent time thinking about the ways in which this decision resonated with her values.

She wanted a solution that would offer mental peace and not conflict with her avowed stance on financial responsibility.

- Implementation with Integrity: Vidya applied for a consolidation loan. This took all of her existing loans and put them into one loan which had a lower interest rate. The result was that her monthly payment actually went down, but more importantly it simplified the management of her debt which was really weighing on her emotionally.

Increasing Income with Purposeful Side Projects:

- Identifying Meaningful Opportunities: She explored side hustles that not only aligned with my skills but also gave her a sense of purpose and fulfillment. She decided to freelance as a graphic designer and tutor English online; both of these gigs allowed her to work towards helping others while making some extra cash on the side.
- Time Management for Emotional Balance: Juggling her full-time job along with side projects required Vidya to put some thought into managing time. She made a timetable for herself which would help her work on these projects without having to feel overwhelmed and at the same time not losing her mental peace and compromising on her values.

Creating a Budget Rooted in Morality and Self-Care:

- Ethical Planning: She drafted a budget that reflected her values of living within means and paying off debt. She tracked everything she spent and looked for ways to reduce costs without negatively impacting her health or compromising morality.
- Regular Reviews with Mindful Adjustments: She would review her budget regularly and make adjustments as needed. She would never spend without taking into account her emotional spendings or values, she would always review her budget first before making any financial commitment just to be sure it was still within her goals and made sense and when it no longer did made sense to, she won't have any guilt saying no and will move on.

Maintaining Motivation and Emotional Discipline:

- Setting Morally-Aligned Milestones: Vidya knew how to set small, morally aligned milestones in her journey of coming out of debt. She celebrated it, not just for the money progress but the emotional strength and integrity she achieved.
- Support System for Emotional and Moral Strength: Vidya reached out to her friends and family for emotional support. She used this

interaction as a tool to sustain her journey, and to increase the emotional strength and be accountable towards what she intended to achieve.

Results: Over a period of two years, Vidya's emphasis on emotional well-being and morality led to some astounding results:

Debt Reduction: Vidya successfully managed to pay out 70% of her student loan debt within 1 year. And she did it all by maintaining her emotional and moral integrity.

- Emotional Confidence: The fact that by sticking to her budget, and adding more income streams, she'd not only improved her financial world but also made herself feel better about being in control of her life.
- Future Planning with Moral Clarity: With substantial reduction in debt, Vidya could begin to look at future oriented financial goals such as saving for emergency and retirement in a larger context of making ethical choices and emotional well-being.

Vidya's journey is a reflection of the fact that if we can align our financial choices with our emotional well-being and moral compass, financial constraints can be managed without compromising on peace and values. Her story tells us that it is important to achieve one's financial goals but not at the cost of emotional and moral bankruptcy.

Are Morals Malleable?

Morals, the principles we use to guide our understanding of right and wrong, often feel like indestructible truths woven into the fabric of our lives. They're the solid foundation upon which we make decisions, form relationships, and construct our identities. But are they really unchangeable? Are morals the one aspect of humanity immune to shifts in perspective and influence from the world around us?

Morals are a mix of our inborn intuition, feelings and values constructed through experiences and external factors. While some aspects of our morality feel as if they are written in stone within us, there is a good reason to believe that morals can change as we do due to the many fluctuations that occur throughout our lives.

Some morals seem to be inherent, perhaps because they are based on our evolutionary instincts or because we were exposed to them during early stages of our childhood. Our innate understanding about concepts such as fairness or our aversion to cause unnecessary harm can be considered as examples for such universal morals. However, most of the morals that we hold are acquired through culture, education and personal experience. And these morals tend to be more malleable and adjust themselves based on new information or changed circumstances.

Let's imagine a child growing up in a community where sharing is highly valued. This child might come to have a strong moral belief in generosity. But then, as an adult, they meet people in other contexts that feel quite different —university or the workplace, for example— where they see that it can be rewarding to withhold resources. In such cases, we might expect them to re-evaluate how generality applies.

Factors Contributing to Moral Malleability

Morals aren't something that exist in isolation; they're constantly being formed and reformed by different external and internal factors. We've covered this in one of the earlier chapters, but I'm mentioning this again, so you can realize that these things will also let us understand how our moral compass is a fluidic thing.

- Cultural and Social Influences

  Society plays a vital role in moulding our Morality. From the childhood itself, Individual is born into a Society which binds them into relationships and at same time teaches them to be behave properly in the Society. The Community to which we belong, together with the social, religious and educational institutions, have a large influence on our moral conduct.

In the past, society thought that many things were okay. Like how it was considered acceptable to have strict gender roles. But as we have become more knowledgeable and aware of gender equality, we have realized that those standards of what is "right" were wrong. So, someone who thinks their ways of doing something is morally "right", might just be closed-minded, ignorant and wrong.

- Personal Experiences

  Our experiences – especially when it comes to grappling with tough emotional or ethical issues – can transform our moral convictions. Trauma, deep loss or a life-altering event frequently leads people to question their existing moral positions.

  Someone who has a loved one killed by violent crime may come to be firmly in favour of justice or retribution, where before they may have been more forgiving. This perspective change reflects reaction to personal experience; their morals were obviously up for grabs.

- Education and Knowledge

  Such encounters provide not only the latest ideas, philosophies, and knowledge, but also transform our morals. The more we come to know about the world and acquire thorough insight in different perspectives of life the more possible is that our moral code will be changing.

A person who grew up knowing only a small corner of the world, maybe in a town without much diversity, might have some strongly prejudiced opinions. But someone who was taught about other cultures in school or who travelled extensively would have a more inclusive and tolerant moral outlook instead, revealing how malleable morals can be with information.

- Relationships and Social Connections

  The people we are closest to — family, friends, mentors and even adversaries — can strongly impact our morals. Relationships force us to encounter perspectives different from our own and can lead us to change or even abandon previous moral assumptions.

Someone who enters into a romantic relationship with a person from another culture may notice that their existing morals begin to evolve under the impact of an unfamiliar set of values. They might, for example, become either more tolerant of religious diversity or more fundamentalist and rigid in their faith if their partner is from a different religious background.

Moral should be reserved but they can be malleable. But it is necessary to be a constant and not to forget that the cause makes you to start. People with rigid morals become inflexible, they won't change their minds under any condition – such people have no future because the nature of the environment is changing. On the other hand, if your moral is too flexible, you'll lose an identity or you won't have integrity.

It's important to have a consistent moral foundation because it provides stability and normalcy. It requires self-assuredness in your decisions, knowing you're acting on what you truly believe.

A person who constantly values honesty will have less trouble navigating through difficult times, because they don't have to take the time to figure out where they stand on being honest. They know and it gives them clarity in hard situations.

It is important to be open for the changing of morals as well. Adaptability means that a person takes new information, new circumstances, and changed cultural ethics into consideration without losing their own focus.

Someone that changes their morals on environmental responsibility because of global warming shows how changing morals can have an upside for moral progress.

How Morals Change as We Grow Up

As we navigate our way through life, our moral convictions shift, whether it's the clear-cut perceptions of right and wrong during childhood, or the more refined and intricate sense of morality which develops as we enter adulthood. Our understanding of how and why this occurs is discussed in this chapter, including an investigation into the stages of moral development and the determining factors behind our transformations.

Childhood: The Formation of Basic Morals

Our moral sense is built, and not just evolved; it's built in childhood under the influence of the people and circumstances of our early lives. Parents, of course, are often what we have in mind when we think about who shapes a child's moral compass, but parents have almost certainly never been the sole or even primary influence.

Imitation and Internalization: Young children begin to learn about right and wrong before they even turn two by watching, imitating, and eventually internalizing the behavior of parents and other adults around them. So-called moral norms are in this way "built in" to their moral cognitive capacities.

A child seeing their parents help a neighbour in need, for example, might learn that it's good to be kind and generous and begin to form their own moral ideas based on that.

Rule-Based Morality: When we're children, we tend to think of morals in a rule-based way. We see rules as fixed and unchanging and put a premium on being obedient and avoiding punishment. This kind of black-and-white thinking is normal for early moral reasoning.

A child might think that lying is always wrong because it's a rule, and they haven't yet figured out that there are situations in which telling the truth can cause harm (such is the simplicity of their moral reasoning).

Adolescence: Questioning and Reevaluating Morals

Children in adolescence begin to doubt the moral codes they were raised with. The doubting is part of a process of becoming more independent and developing one's own view, not one that necessarily rejects one's earlier view, but questions it.

Moral Flexibility: Adolescents begin to question moral absolutes and may challenge the notion that morality and ethics are, in fact, absolute. They see that there can be conflicting ethical and moral opinions about issues, especially those for which there is no clear-cut answer.

A teenager may begin to question the rigid moral norms they were brought up with, for example, the idea that it is always wrong to disobey. They encounter situations in which it seems right to break a norm—they may need to defy an unfair adult or institution—so they think again.

Peer Influence: In adolescence, peers play a large role in the moral development. The need to belong and be accepted by one's friends may cause the adolescent to pick up new morals that go against their parents or society's authority.

A teenager who becomes friends with a peer group that is focused on activism and social justice causes may develop a strong moral orientation toward those issues, regardless of the emphasis placed on them in the teenager's home environment—and indeed, this may lead them to change their sense of what their moral priorities should be.

Adulthood: Integrating Experience and Morality

In adulthood, moral development continues as people deal with real life and work through moral dilemmas in day-to-day life. Moral beliefs are also part of the crystallized self-concept and identity.

Life Experiences: The morals that adults hold, are often influenced by the experiences of life that they have had; their career, marriage, raising children, and losing loved ones. These situations offer chances to mature one's morals and come to a deeper understanding of moral truths.

A person who faces a career setback due to unethical behavior in their field may be spurred to become more dedicated to integrity and transparency. The moral transition is a response to one's professional context.

Moral Autonomy: One further way that adults can be more moral than children is that they can, in seeking to live up to the moral standards they are aware of, strive for what Rousseau calls "moral autonomy." As we noted in regarding justice above, the development of reason and language allows us to reflect upon and understand the reasons underlying our behaviors and habits. Some of these we will see to be good reasons; others will seem less compelling. When this happens, we come to develop a notion of how we ought to behave - based on reasons that we ourselves accept as reasonable or rational.

An adult who has chosen to volunteer for a cause they believe in, despite disapproval from either society or their family, is using moral autonomy. Their decision was based on a commitment to personal morality, rather than compliance with external norms.

Balancing Moral Complexity: Adulthood tends to include an appreciation for how complicated morality can be. Adults often find themselves in ethical dilemmas, and they frequently recognize that different moral values are at stake and that their possible courses of action could have costs and consequences.

Example: An honesty-loving parent who also values the feelings of their child might be in a dilemma whether to tell him/her a painful fact

The question of whether morals can change or not is a difficult and important one. Some people might think that certain moral questions are easy — surely it is obvious to all well-intentioned, right-minded people that slavery is wrong, for example? But the evidence seems to suggest that simple though it may be, our sureness about our own moral beliefs simply doesn't make them static. Instead, our experience tells us what common sense might have suggested: that they are formed by early experience and cultural influence, shaped by education and conversation (and argument), and grow and develop or wither on the vine with neglect.

As we grow, our morals are put to the test and we learn that the world is not so easily divided into good people and bad people. The transition from the absolutist morality of children to the nuanced moral reasoning of grown-ups shows that our moral convictions are not innate. They're developed and deepened over a lifetime.

Ultimately, the fact that morals can change is not a weakness at all. It's what allows us to grow and become more empathetic, to respond to the world we live in with relevance and compassion. Striking a balance between embracing that—while maintaining integrity and consistency—is really how we can live our most moral lives.

Case Study

Rakesh's Journey to Financial Stability

Rakesh, 32, a software engineer was at crossroads of his career given the changing technology landscape and possible job changes. While future prospects were unstable, Rakesh knew it was an imperative to be financially secure. He wanted to build an emergency corpus to have the much-needed peace of mind and also the flexibility to take career related decisions without having the fear of feeling financially insecure. In this process, Rakesh would constantly be questioning if his pursuit of financial stability is in line with his values or would he discover that values change as we make progress.

Challenge: Primary challenge that Rakesh had in this context was to ensure that he had enough of savings to sustain for 6 months without salary, which he considered as an emergency fund use through transition/unforeseen situation without having to compromise on integrity.

Solution: You approach Financial Prudence with Moral Reflection. Can you change your moral values as they are challenged by financial success or should they remain constant?

- He set aside money each month but also dreamed up ways he could use it if there was an emergency to justify tapping into the fund.

Setting a Clear Goal with Moral Clarity:

- Save a Target Amount considering your Expenses: Rakesh calculated his monthly expenses and targeted to save enough for six months, which amounted to INR 1,50,000. He made sure his savings didn't hamper doing things he believed in like supporting charities or financing family emergencies.
- Action Plan Aligned with Values: He developed a detailed plan to achieve this target within one year, ensuring that every financial decision he made was in alignment with his core values.

Creating a Budget with Ethical Reflection:

- Expense Tracking with Moral Insight: Rakesh kept an account of all his expenses and made sure that whatever he spent, it was in line with his moral values. He cut down everything that he thought was luxury but continued giving contributions to charity.
- Savings Allocation with Integrity: Every month, he set aside a fixed percentage of his salary to his emergency fund and made sure that he achieved his savings targets while also being true to his moral obligations.

Implementing Discipline while Questioning Moral Flexibility:

- Automatic Transfers with Moral Deliberation: After setting up automatic transfers to a high-yield savings account for his emergency fund, Rakesh wondered whether he might be able to practice more consistent savings if his financial discipline became less consciously engaged and less morally laden.

- Avoiding Temptations with Ethical Considerations: Rakesh taught himself not to go for things which he can manage without, and always thinking if his moral compass could adjust to rationalize such expenses or he should continue to be led by his principles.

Monitoring Progress with Moral Reflection:

- Regular Reviews with Moral Introspection: Every month, Rakesh would review and if needed make changes to his budget. He would ask himself whether these changes are still acceptable as per his moral values or not. Are you indirectly compromising your moral values in your pursuit of financial freedom?

  Results: After a year, Rakesh did build his six-month emergency fund but not without asking himself along the way if he had to compromise on his values. Here are the results:

- Financial Peace of Mind: The emergency fund gave Rakesh a lot of peace of mind. He knew that he had an umbrella ready in case there was a sudden rain or if he decided to change his career. Was this peace of mind worth any moral compromises?

- Career Flexibility with Moral Integrity: Rakesh found it easier to explore new careers and even contemplate a job change or further education, all the while not losing sight of what he felt was morally right.
- Overall Stability and Moral Awareness: While the fund had given him financial stability, it also made Rakesh wonder if his morals were still as unyielding as they once were or if they had been moulded with the pursuit of his ambition.

Rakesh's story exemplifies the importance of Financial Prudence and Moral Reflection. Rakesh established financial goals, developed and stuck to a budget, saved religiously; all of these demonstrated that financial well-being can be attained through thoughtful planning alone. But Rakesh's narrative also poses several interrelated mysteries about how our financial goals interact with ethics in life. Are our ethical commitments firm enough? What happens when we feel they are not?

Deep Dive into Introspection

What are my core values when it comes to money?

Knowing what you truly value when it comes to money is the first step toward creating a financial life that reflects your most important goals and dreams. Your values are the building blocks for the choices you make every day with your money, from how you earn, spend, and save to how you invest and give it away. Understanding where your own core values lie in your financial life can help you make smarter decisions and find more happiness and contentment in work, spending, saving, and giving.

At its core, money is a tool we use to navigate the world, to further our goals, and to take care of ourselves and those we love. And the way we wield this tool is deeply influenced by our core values. These values act as a Guiding Star that helps us make decisions with our money on a daily basis. When our financial actions are in alignment with those values, we experience a sense of ease and fulfillment in our financial lives. But when there's dissonance between what we hold dear and how we're actually behaving around money, it doesn't matter how much money you have—a deep sense of "something's not right" will continue to irritate.

Why Core Values Matter in Financial Decisions

The principles and beliefs that we consider most important in our lives are our core values. They determine who we are and what we stand for. With matters of money, our core values affect how we view wealth, how we spend money, how we save, and how we invest money. For example, if you value security, you probably are inclined to making sure you have a big emergency fund saved up as well as investing into low-risk assets like government bonds etc. versus someone who is looking for growth that may take more calculated risks with the stock market or starting a business.

Knowing your core values helps to create a financial game plan that represents the real you. The relationship between what you value most and where you dedicate your money should be synonymous with each other if not it'll just lead to financial success without much fulfillment, and in challenging times it won't bring you a sense of ease.

Reflecting on your core values can be tough because **it requires you to be brutally honest with yourself**. It forces you to look in the mirror and ask yourself some difficult questions about what really matters most to you. Do you value security more than freedom? Is giving a bigger source of joy for you than growing and becoming more? There are no right or wrong answers, there's only what's true for you.

This is a process, not a one-time event. Your values will change over time. Likely, your objectives and implementation strategies will change with them. Revisiting what you care about most on a some-what regular basis allows you to make course corrections when necessary.

Reflecting on Core Values

1. Security:

For many people, financial security is a primary value. It represents the peace of mind that comes from knowing you have enough resources to handle life's uncertainties. Whether it's building an emergency fund, having insurance, or saving for retirement, security-driven individuals prioritize stability and risk management in their financial planning.

Exercise: Note down the answers for yourself

- Do you prioritize having a safety net in place for unexpected events?
- How much of your financial decision-making is influenced by the need to feel secure?
- Are you willing to sacrifice potential gains for the assurance that your financial base is solid?

2. Freedom:

Financial freedom is the ability to live life on your own terms, without being constrained by financial limitations. This value emphasizes the importance of having choices—whether it's the freedom to retire early, travel extensively, pursue passions, or simply not be tied down by debt.

Exercise: Note down the answers for yourself

- How important is it to you to have control over your time and lifestyle?
- Are you willing to take financial risks in exchange for the possibility of greater freedom?
- What sacrifices are you prepared to make now to achieve financial well-being later?

3. Generosity:

For those who value generosity, money is seen as a tool for making a positive impact on others. This could involve charitable giving, supporting family and friends, or contributing to causes you believe in. Generosity-driven individuals often find fulfillment in using their resources to benefit others.

Exercise: Note down the answers for yourself

- How much do you prioritize giving or helping others with your financial resources?
- Does the act of giving bring you satisfaction and a sense of purpose?
- Are you comfortable with the balance between your giving and your financial needs?

4. Growth:

If growth is a core value for you, then you likely view money as a means to expand your opportunities and improve your life. This could include investing in education, starting a business, or continuously seeking ways to increase your wealth. Growth-oriented individuals often focus on wealth-building strategies and personal development.

Exercise: Note down the answers for yourself

- How important is it for you to see your financial resources grow over time?
- Are you willing to take calculated risks to achieve greater financial rewards?
- Do you prioritize reinvesting your earnings into further opportunities for growth?

5. Simplicity:

Simplicity as a core value emphasizes living a life that is uncluttered and free from unnecessary financial complications. This could mean minimizing debt, avoiding material excess, or adopting a minimalist lifestyle. Simplicity-driven individuals often seek to reduce financial stress by focusing on what truly matters and avoiding distractions.

Exercise: Note down the answers for yourself

- Do you feel more at ease when your financial life is straightforward and manageable?

- Are you inclined to minimize your expenses and live within your means?
- How does the pursuit of simplicity impact your financial goals and decisions?

6. Success:

For some, financial success is a reflection of their hard work, ambition, and accomplishments. It represents the achievement of goals, the accumulation of wealth, and the recognition that comes with it. Success-oriented individuals often set high financial targets and strive to reach them through career advancement, entrepreneurship, or strategic investments.

Exercise: Note down the answers for yourself

- How do you define financial success for yourself?
- Are you driven by the desire to achieve specific financial milestones or status?
- What are you willing to do to achieve the financial success you envision?

7. Contentment:

Contentment is the value of being satisfied with what you have, regardless of how much or how little that may be. It's about finding peace and happiness in your current financial situation and resisting the urge to constantly strive for more. Contentment-driven individuals often focus on gratitude and mindful living, rather than the pursuit of wealth.

Exercise: Note down the answers for yourself

- Do you find joy in your current financial circumstances, without constantly seeking more?
- How does contentment shape your financial choices and priorities?
- Are you comfortable with the balance between ambition and satisfaction in your financial life?

To help you discover what your core values are when it comes to money, you'll need to take a look back at some of the financial decisions you've made in your life so far and the emotions that went along with them. Here's how:

- Analyse what you liked about past financial decisions. What made them important and meaningful to you? If you can identify the underlying values, you can often find new ways to live those values more fully without needing to spend more money. Decisions you value are much easier to stick with in the long run.
- Evaluate where you are financially. Do an inventory of your current financial position. Are you contented with your current position? If no, which of the fundamental values do you fail to satisfy? This can enable you pinpoint areas in which your financial life may not be in accord with your values.
- Consider Future Goals. Next, think about the financial goals you want to set down the road. What do you want to achieve? How is it going to

be possible for those things to happen if you don't have a solid financial foundation, which is your current situation? What are those goals telling you what type of person, what type of investor, and what type of earner you need to become in order to reach those goals?

- Seek Clarity. Take time to write about what really counts in your life and in money to you. Use the questions provided under each purpose to spark your reflection and see how it applies to your life. This self-inquiry will help you better understand what is driving you financially.

Exercise:

1. How do my moral beliefs influence my financial decisions? Assess and list down how your values shape your spending, saving, investing, and giving habits.
2. Am I satisfied with my current financial situation?
3. Evaluate whether your financial life aligns with your moral beliefs and if there are areas where you feel conflicted or unfulfilled.
4. What changes can I make to better align my finances with my values?

Building Your Financial Foundation

After you are able to identify your core values which are transparent everything will be fine with you without any doubt, so it is just the time for you to start managing your money in a way that supports these principles. It is this foundation that constitutes the very basis of your financial life gradually building stability and security yet affording ample opportunities for development and versatility.

Following are the fundamental steps of laying down a financial backbone according to your core values:

1. Identify Your Core Values: Begin by thinking about the values you hold that have influenced money choices in your past. How might they impact decisions going forward?

2. Set Clear Financial Goals: Make sure your financial goals are connected to what you value most. If security is a top value, your goals may include saving for emergencies, eliminating debt, and investing in stable, low-risk investments. If freedom is what you prize most, your goals may revolve around achieving financial well-being and creating multiple streams of income. [You can reach out to me for help on making those goals clearer]

3. Create a Budget That Reflects Your Values: Your budget should be a reflection of what is most important to you in life. Allocate your money towards your goals and what matters most. If giving is a high priority, make sure you budget in giving or helping others. If growth is a value, you hold dearly, make sure you are putting money aside for learning,

classes, coaches and/or investing in yourself or business.

4. Invest in What You Value: Let your investments reflect what is important to you. For example, if simplicity is important, you would want to use low-cost index funds or some other simple type of investment. If success were what was most important to you, you would look for higher returns even if the investments were riskier.

5. Revisit Regularly: As with anything in life, it is likely that your core values and financial goals will change over time. Schedule regular visits to make sure you are giving to what's important to you now–not who you used to be. This will help you keep your financial house in order as well as keep the real you alive and thriving.

Phew!

Having now looked at the entirety of morality, we can see how everything is so deeply connected. Our principles are all intertwined, and every decision we make creates ripples across every part of our lives. So, as we zoom back in on financial well-being with this newfound clarity, we can start to apply these lessons and live more intentionally and honestly in regards to money.

As we start to enjoy financial freedom again, it's important to rethink the moral compass that guides our financial choices. Expanding our perspective on morality helps us modify that compass so our personal wealth goals include becoming the best people we can be.

A person is no longer just using their financial well-being as a means to personal freedom, but they can now contribute to their community. In this context, the target of financial well-being is no longer self-centred for one's own good, but rather moralised as what is good for one can be spread among many.

Applying Broader Moral Lessons to Financial well-being

The study of ethics outside of finance has yielded results that can boost our pursuit of financial freedom. The words empathy, integrity, or justice would sound strange and meaningless if they were not translated down into the world of personal finance from the abstract universe they inhabit.

Consider the virtue of empathy. At a higher moral plane, empathy means the capacity to understand and feel the other person's feelings. If we were to apply this concept to money, it would mean that we should consider the feelings related to our money decisions on others and how those decisions shape their well-being. We should consider whether our spending decisions support worthy causes, whether our investing choices assist others in making and keeping more of their money (e.g., by backing socially responsible companies or green energy initiatives), or whether we're using a portion of what we have to help those in need. In these ways, empathy ensures that our pursuit of independence doesn't come at others' expense.

Redefining Financial Success

With a broader moral perspective, we can redefine financial success. Financial success is not simply the money and wealth we accumulate; it is also the money and wealth that reflects our moral values. This definition suggests a somewhat more complete approach to striving for financial well-being in which the pursuit of our financial goals is consistent with our living a more morally worthy life.

A business owner focused on environmental stewardship might expand a definition of financial success to encompass not only profitability, but the sustainability of business practices. By tying financial goals to values that reflect a moral commitment, a congratulatory sentiment can be achieved on multiple fronts.

Ultimately, the return to financial well-being, with a broader view of morality, reminds me that this path is not a self-indulgent pursuit — it is a MORAL QUEST. Every financial choice is a chance to put our money where our mouth is, live in alignment with our values, and help make this world better for everyone.

A person who believes financial well-being is a moral imperative might just choose to pay off their debts not only for the sake of being free themselves, but because they believe in fulfilling obligations, they want to set an example of integrity and responsibility or they simply feel it's their duty to help others. This elevates financial freedom from becoming a thing you pursue to something you are on a crusade for.

By including the insights gained from a wider investigation into morality, we can come to the path of financial well-being afresh. Along this path, we simultaneously build a future, and thereby a life, that expresses our highest values and integrates what we would like to achieve financially with who we would like to be morally.

Actionable Insights!

Understanding in theory what financial morality is, and effectively applying it in practice are two different things. Actionable insights help to bridge that gap by giving you clear and practical guidance for aligning your financial life with your own sense of what's right and wrong.

In this chapter we will spend some time reflecting on your awareness and knowledge about yourself, with particular emphasis on the way in which your values and beliefs shape the financial choices that you make. The purpose of this self-reflection is to give you a clearer sense of your guiding principles and how congruent they are with your financial behaviours.

Instructions

- Find a Quiet Space: Find a quiet comfortable distraction free space where you can concentrate. Keep a notebook ready for your answers.
- Time Yourself- Allocate an amount of time for each section of the exercise, e.g. 15-20 minutes a section to ensure you reflect on all points.
- To avoid generalities, say honesty and details are required when you answer the questions. The more detailed your explanations the more insightful your reflections will be.

Self-Reflection on Values and Beliefs

1. Core Values and Beliefs
    - What core values and beliefs guide your life decisions?
    - Describe how these values have influenced your choices in the past.
2. Moral Dilemmas
    - Reflect on a time when you faced a moral dilemma. How did your values influence your decision, and what was the outcome?
3. Conflict Resolution
    - How do you reconcile any conflicts between your personal values and external expectations or pressures?

Insights on Financial Decisions

1. Recent Financial Decisions
    - Analyse a recent financial decision you made. How did your moral beliefs impact this decision?
2. Alignment with Values
    - Identify any areas where your financial practices might not align with your core values. What changes could you make to better align your financial behavior with your morals?

3. Cultural and Personal Influences

    - Reflect on how your cultural, religious, or personal beliefs shape your approach to money management and financial goals.

Personal and Professional Alignment

1. Goals and Values

    - Consider your personal and professional goals. How do these goals align with your moral principles? Are there any discrepancies?

2. Work Reflection

    - Think about your current career or business. How does your work reflect your values, and where might improvements be made?

3. Setting Goals

    - Set specific goals for integrating your moral beliefs into your personal and professional life. What steps can you take to achieve these goals?

Action Plan and Commitment

1. Actionable Steps

    - Based on your reflections, list actionable steps you can take to better align your financial practices and life decisions with your values.

2. Timeline for Implementation
    - Create a timeline for implementing these steps. What immediate actions can you take, and what longer-term changes will you plan for?
3. Support Systems
    - Identify any resources or support systems you may need to help you achieve your goals. This could include financial advisors, mentors, or educational resources.

Path to Financial well-being

Many people have the dream of being financially independent— this is not just about having a lot of money; it's about living without financial worries, supporting yourself and your loved ones without needing to rely on others. As depicted earlier, though this objective may appear purely financial savvy, it carries immense moral values in its achievement. Let's now look into detail how those values can be your pathfinders on your way to the financial well-being.

The Foundation of Trust and Integrity

Trust is the foundation of any successful relationship, and in finance, it's no different. Whether you have a job, run a business or are investing, people have to believe in you. That belief is based upon integrity – a core human truth that means we say and do the same things behind closed doors that we would in public.

- Building a Good Reputation: A reputation based on honesty and integrity is like having a backstage pass. People want to work with, hire, and partner with people they can count on. When you become known as someone who keeps their word, follows through, and treats others fairly – you will create relationships that provide you more opportunities and more financial success.

- Long-Term Success: Shortcuts or unethical behavior may seem to give an immediate boost but they are sure to be harmful in the long run. A person who cheats or lies in business may achieve short term financial gains but eventually lose trust and face serious repercussions that will adversely affect their financial future. Acting with integrity helps build a steady foundation for successful relationships.

Responsibility and Financial Discipline

To become financially independent, you must take the following steps. It also requires making a few adjustments to your lifestyle. This can be seen as responsible actions which will help to get you there. Strive for financial well-being with serious effort and smart work along with careful spending.

- Budgeting and Saving: Responsible money management involves the creation of a budget as well as following it. Budget helps you to live within your means, avoid unnecessary debt and save for the future. To put a premium on saving rather than spending on non-essentials is a responsible decision that aligns you with financial well-being.

- Investing Wisely: Responsibility also means making smart choices about how to grow your money. That involves doing your homework, knowing what you're getting into, and not making impulsive decisions that could put your financial security at risk. Being a responsible investor requires patience and self-discipline—two things that breed responsibility.

Living beyond your means by borrowing can only land you in financial soup. Being a responsible manager of your finances helps you keep debt as low as possible always striving to lower it further. This reduces financial worries and helps you build on wealth over time.

Case Study

Komal's Balanced Approach to Wealth Building

Komal- 38 years, IT manager. Over the years she saw steady growth in income due to promotions and successful project execution. But she kept her life style very simple. The mantra being 'Simplicity and Financial Discipline'.

Challenge: Komal faced several challenges:

- Managing Increased Income: With her increased income she had to be sure that her lifestyle didn't inflate and that took some strong Self Discipline.
- Balancing Lifestyle and Savings: Keeping a moderate lifestyle and at the same time investing most of her earning in the right resources needed good knowledge on managing money.
- Avoiding Lifestyle Inflation: Komal had to avoid the common mistake of getting used to a better lifestyle with each increase in income.

Solution: Komal embodied 'Simplicity and Financial Discipline' throughout her approach in managing increased Income. Let's see how she kept a balance and made it successful financially.

Maintaining a Modest Lifestyle:

- Budget Adherence: Komal had been sticking to a budget which focused on needs and not splurging on unnecessary things. She stayed in a small home and used to drive a car with good mileage as she believed in the principle of simple living.

- Mindful Spending: She made sure to spend her money on things that had value and practicality instead of luxury. She didn't buy things on an impulse and made financially wise decisions.

Focusing on Savings:

- Automated Savings: Komal automated her savings transfers to make sure that a big chunk of her salary got saved each month, religiously.
- Emergency Fund: She created and preserved a strong emergency fund of around six months of living costs to have economic security and serenity.

Strategic Investing:

- Diversified Investments: Komal had put her money in a mix of stocks, bonds and mutual funds. She had tried to cover all strategies of being risky but having a potential to grow also over the time.
- Long-Term Goals: She made sure that her investments aligned with the long-term financial goals she set, which were retirement savings, wealth accumulation and financial well-being.

Avoiding Lifestyle Inflation:

- Goal-Oriented: Komal kept in mind her financial goals and did not get carried away with increase in income leading to increase in spend.
- Reinvesting Gains: She chose to reinvest her earnings back into her savings and investment accounts, rather than increasing her discretionary spending – in essence, two days of the week she was actually working for the future.

Results: Komal's disciplined approach led to:

- Enhanced Savings: A large part of her earning was saved over the years due to her resolve to live a simple life. Consequently, she had built up considerable financial reserves.
- Strong Investment Growth: She made some really smart investments that have guaranteed great returns in the long-term.
- Financial Security and Fulfillment: This was a strategy that gave her financial security. She knew she wasn't compromising values and she knew she was building wealth responsibly.

We can easily notice how despite doubling her income Komal continued to maintain a similar lifestyle. The thumb rule is to focus more on increasing our savings and investments, rather than our lifestyle with the increase in incomes. Simplicity and one's core values be the bedrock for success to achieve financial freedom.

Respect for Self and Others

How you perceive yourself and others when it comes to financial well-being is also linked to respect.

- Self-Worth and Earning: If you respect yourself, you'll know the worth of your work and skills. You'll charge what you're worth and not settle for less. This is one of the cornerstones in building a financial fortress reflective of your worth.
- Respecting Others' Time and Efforts: If you respect your work, you must also respect the work of others. This means paying fair wages. It also means being on time and fulfilling commitments. When you do what you say you will do (and other people feel they are being treated fairly), they will support you in return by doing what they say they will do. This builds positive relationships that support your financial goals.

Compassion and Generosity

Financial well-being does not only speak about the assurance of your tomorrow, but also describes how you can use your wealth to support others. Compassion and generosity are ethical values that might make one's financial journey much more interesting.

- Supporting Others: When you assist others through your financial success such as charity, helping a friend or investing in your community you create an impact that is greater than your own personal gains. It also offers personal satisfaction and strengthens your relationships with others.
- The Law of Reciprocity: The more you give, the more that comes back to you in all kinds of ways. Whether it's through new connections, partnerships or just goodwill, giving can open doors that lead to an even greater level of financial well-being.

Case Study

Bharat's Journey to Fulfillment Through Charity

Bharat, a 45-year-old businessman and entrepreneur had made a lot of money over the years. But as we went along in his coaching process, he realized that despite all the professional success, something was missing in life. He wanted to experience something deeper and more fulfilling but did not know what or how. Bharat decided to start a charitable fund with the goal of giving back to society in some meaningful way. His story highlights the importance of 'Generosity and Purposeful living'.

Challenge: Bharat faced the challenge of:

- Finding a Purpose Beyond Wealth: His financial success, while important to him, wasn't enough of a calling for him or reflective of what he believed was his ability to contribute.
- To Make a Lasting Impression: The setup and management of a charitable fund called for meticulous preparation and a dedication to make sure that the fund will have an impact

Bharat lived Generosity and Purposeful Living in his Philanthropy. Here is how he actually started and operated his charitable foundation:

Setting Up the Charitable Fund:

- Defining the Purpose: Bharat identified the causes which were important for him i.e.

education, healthcare and poverty mitigation, and he established the charitable fund with specific objectives and a mission to address those causes.

- Initial Contribution: At the outset, he contributed significantly to ensure that the corpus was substantial enough to make an impact from day one. Additionally, Bharat committed to provide annual contributions to help maintain the corpus of the fund.

Strategic Planning and Management:

- Research and Collaboration: Bharat did extensive research to find out the right organizations and efforts that can match with his fund's goals. He worked with some experts and leaders from local communities to guide him on how to deploy the fund well.
- Monitoring and Evaluation: He developed the capacity to monitor the impact of the fund, implemented ongoing reviews of outcomes and fine-tuned processes for maximizing the efficiency in fund deployment.

Personal Engagement:

- Active Involvement: Bharat was actively involved in the initiatives of the fund and interacted with both beneficiaries and volunteers which gave him first-hand view of the impact of the fund and also helped him relate to the cause personally.

- Sharing the Vision: He invited others to participate and help the fund achieve its mission, building a community of peers who shared his passion for impact.

Experiencing Fulfillment:

- Impact and Satisfaction: The success of the charitable fund provided Bharat with deep impact and fulfillment. Seeing the change in his community and hearing stories of changed lives strengthened his resolve to continue giving back.
- Long-Term Legacy: Bharat's charitable fund became something that would live beyond him, to be a reflection of who he was and what was important to him.

Bharat's establishment of the charitable fund led to:

- Positive Community Impact: The fund has supported many activities including education scholarships, medical help and support to families of below poverty line, which has resulted in overall improvement in the community.
- Personal Fulfillment: Bharat gained immense satisfaction and a sense of purpose by using his wealth for a cause.
- Inspiration to Others: His philanthropic drive encouraged others to participate in the charity event thereby increasing the positive effect in the society.

The more I heard about Bharat's charitable fund and his literal investment in social good, I was sure that there was something interesting in his motives. When you realise that value is not only about creating wealth but also distributing it and that true wealth doesn't become lesser if you give some of it away, you have struck GOLD!

"Remember that the happiest people are not those getting more, but those giving more." — H. Jackson Brown Jr.

By adopting the morals like integrity, responsibility, fairness, respect and compassion you build a strong base for successful journey of finance and money as well. So, take your morals along with you in your long journey of life to experience this beautiful world with all its perks by becoming financially independent.

Exercise:

Using this chapter as a reference, reflect on how each moral value influences your financial decisions. Write down how integrity, responsibility, fairness, respect, and compassion impact your financial choices.

1. Integrity:

2. Responsibility:

3. Fairness:

4. Respect:

5. Compassion:

Moral Wealth Creation

In a world where wealth is often pursued at any cost, the concept of Moral wealth creation stands as a beacon of integrity. Building wealth is not just about accumulating money; it's about doing so in a way that aligns with our moral values. For readers in India, where cultural and spiritual values hold significant importance, this chapter explores strategies for creating wealth that is not only abundant but also Morally sound.

Understanding Moral Wealth Creation

Moral wealth creation involves making financial decisions that reflect honesty, fairness, and respect for others. It's about ensuring that the methods we use to build wealth do not harm others or compromise our principles.

Wealth in India has always been seen as more than just material accumulation. The concept of *Artha*—the pursuit of wealth—is one of the four Purusharthas, or goals of life, according to Hindu philosophy. It is balanced with *Dharma* (righteousness), *Kama* (desire), and *Moksha* (liberation). This ancient framework underscores the idea that wealth should be pursued with integrity and used for the greater good.

The *Arthashastra*, an ancient Indian treatise on statecraft, economic policy, and military strategy, written by Kautilya (Chanakya), offers insights into the Moral management of wealth. It emphasizes the importance of righteous governance, fair trade, and the Moral use of resources. For instance, it advises rulers to avoid exploitation of the poor and to ensure that wealth is distributed in a way that benefits society as a whole.

Example: In modern times, this philosophy is reflected in the way some Indian businesses operate. The Tata Group, one of India's largest conglomerates, has a longstanding commitment to Moral business practices. They have consistently reinvested a significant portion of their profits back into the community through charitable trusts, supporting education, healthcare, and rural development. This approach aligns with the traditional Indian view that wealth should serve a higher purpose.

Moral wealth creation involves accumulating wealth through methods that are consistent with moral and Moral standards. It is about making financial decisions that not only benefit you but also contribute positively to society. This concept goes beyond mere compliance with the law; it requires a commitment to doing what is right, even when it might be more profitable to take shortcuts.

Example: Moral wealth creation can be seen in the practices of socially responsible businesses. Amul, the Indian dairy cooperative, is a prime example. Established in 1946, Amul was created to empower farmers and ensure they received fair prices for their milk. The cooperative model has been hugely successful, making Amul one of the largest food brands in India while uplifting millions of rural farmers. The success of Amul demonstrates how Moral practices can lead to sustainable and significant wealth creation.

Aligning Investments with Values

1. Socially Responsible Investing (SRI):

   Socially Responsible Investing (SRI) is an investment strategy that seeks to generate financial returns while also considering social, environmental, and governance (ESG) factors. In India, SRI has gained momentum as investors become more aware of the impact their money can have on society and the environment.

   Example: The SBI Magnum Equity ESG Fund is one of the prominent SRI options in India. It focuses on investing in companies that score highly on ESG criteria. This fund has attracted investors who are not only interested in financial returns but also in contributing to a sustainable future. By choosing SRI, investors can align their portfolios with their Moral values, ensuring that their wealth contributes to positive social outcomes.

2. ESG Criteria:

   Environmental, Social, and Governance (ESG) criteria provide a framework for evaluating the

Moral impact of investments. Companies that perform well on ESG criteria are seen as better long-term investments because they are likely to be more sustainable and resilient.

Example: Infosys, a global leader in technology services, has been a pioneer in embracing ESG principles. Infosys has made significant strides in reducing its carbon footprint, promoting diversity and inclusion, and maintaining strong corporate governance. By investing in companies like Infosys, investors are supporting businesses that are committed to Moral practices.

3. Moral Mutual Funds:

   Moral mutual funds are investment funds that focus on companies adhering to Moral business practices. These funds typically exclude industries like tobacco, alcohol, and weapons, and instead, invest in sectors like renewable energy, healthcare, and education.

   Example: The Tata Moral Fund is one of the oldest and most well-known Moral funds in India. It invests in Shariah-compliant companies, ensuring that the investments adhere to Islamic principles of finance, which prohibit interest-based income and investments in certain prohibited sectors. This fund has performed well over the years, proving that Moral investing can be both morally fulfilling and financially rewarding.

4. Impact Investing:

   Impact investing goes a step further than SRI by actively seeking to create positive social or environmental changes. Impact investors look for opportunities where their capital can have a meaningful impact on society while still generating financial returns.

   Example: The Bharat Innovation Fund is an impact investment fund that focuses on early-stage startups in sectors like healthcare, agriculture, and clean energy. By investing in innovative companies that address critical challenges in India, the Bharat Innovation Fund aims to create both financial returns and significant social impact.

Earning Money through Honest Means

The Importance of Integrity:

Integrity is the cornerstone of Moral wealth creation. Earning money through honest means builds trust, reputation, and long-term success. In India, the Mahabharata offers valuable lessons on integrity and Moral conduct, particularly in the stories of characters like Yudhishthira, who is revered for his commitment to truth and righteousness.

Example: Azim Premji, the founder of Wipro, is widely respected for his Moral leadership. Premji's insistence on transparency, honesty, and Moral business practices has been a guiding principle for Wipro. Even in the face of challenges, Premji has maintained a strong moral compass, ensuring that Wipro remains a trusted and respected company globally.

- Azim Premji and Wipro: Azim Premji transformed Wipro from a small hydrogenated cooking fat company into one of the largest IT services companies in the world. Throughout this journey, Premji remained committed to Moral business practices. He ensured that Wipro adhered to the highest standards of corporate governance and transparency. Today, Wipro is known not only for its technological prowess but also for its commitment to Moral values, which has played a significant role in its long-term success.

- Tata Group: The Tata Group, founded by Jamshedji Tata in 1868, is one of India's oldest and most respected conglomerates. The company's commitment to ethics is evident in its approach to business. For instance, Tata Steel was the first company in the world to introduce an eight-hour workday in 1912, long before labor laws mandated it. The Tata Trusts, which control a majority stake in Tata Sons, the holding company of the Tata Group, reinvest a significant portion of their profits into philanthropic activities, further emphasizing the company's commitment to social well-being.

Moral Dilemmas in Business:

Moral dilemmas are common in business, where the pressure to maximize profits can sometimes lead to moral compromises. However, making the right choice—one that aligns with Moral principles—can lead to long-term success.

Imagine a small business owner who discovers that they can significantly cut costs by outsourcing production to a factory with questionable labor practices. The short-term financial gain is tempting, but the Moral implications are serious. If the business owner chooses to maintain production with Moral suppliers, even at a higher cost, they preserve their integrity and reputation. In the long run, this decision could lead to greater customer loyalty and a more sustainable business model.

Practicing Moral Consumerism

The Power of the Consumer:

Consumers have tremendous power to influence the market by making Moral purchasing decisions. In India, the rise of conscious consumerism is evident in the growing demand for products that are environmentally friendly, socially responsible, and sustainably produced.

Example: The shift towards organic food products in India is a clear indication of this trend. Brands like Organic India and 24 Mantra Organic have gained popularity by offering consumers healthy, pesticide-free options that also support sustainable farming practices. By choosing such products, consumers are not only making healthier choices for themselves but also supporting Moral business practices.

Supporting Local and Sustainable Businesses:

Supporting local and sustainable businesses helps ensure that wealth is distributed more evenly and that small-scale producers, often more aligned with Moral practices, can thrive.

Example: Fabindia, a popular Indian retail brand, focuses on promoting the traditional crafts of India by working with rural artisans. The company sources products directly from over 55,000 craftsmen across India, ensuring they receive fair wages and preserving traditional craft techniques. This business model supports the livelihoods of artisans while offering consumers high-quality, morally produced goods.

Moral Consumption in Everyday Life:

Incorporating Moral consumerism into daily life can be simple yet impactful. It involves making conscious choices about the products we buy, the companies we support, and the way we manage our resources.

Tips for Moral Consumption:

- Choose Eco-Friendly Products: Opt for products with minimal environmental impact, such as those made from recycled materials or that use sustainable packaging.

- Reduce Waste: Practice minimalism by buying only what you need and reducing waste. Reuse and recycle whenever possible.
- Support Fair Trade: Purchase products that are certified as fair trade, ensuring that the workers who made them are paid fairly and work in safe conditions.
- Educate Yourself: Stay informed about the companies you buy from and the practices they follow. Make purchasing decisions that align with your values.

Moral wealth creation is not just about accumulating wealth—it's about doing so in a way that aligns with our values and contributes to the greater good. In India, where cultural and spiritual traditions place a strong emphasis on morality and social responsibility, Moral wealth creation is a path that leads not only to financial success but also to personal fulfillment and social well-being. By integrating Moral principles into our financial strategies, we can build wealth that stands the test of time and serves as a positive force in the world.

Case Study

Nikhil's Journey to Honest Passive Income

Nikhil, a 35-year-old marketing executive, was determined to create additional income streams through honest and ethical means. With a deep passion for writing and sharing knowledge, he decided to start a blog. What began as a simple hobby soon evolved into a significant source of passive income, built on a foundation of integrity and transparency.

Challenge: Nikhil encountered several challenges on his path:

- Building an Audience: Establishing a loyal readership from scratch required significant effort and authenticity.
- Consistency: Balancing regular content updates with his full-time job demanded unwavering dedication and time management.
- Monetization: Finding ethical ways to monetize his blog without compromising its integrity was a critical hurdle.

Solution: Nikhil embraced the principle of "Earning Through Honest Means" throughout his journey. Here's how he transformed his blog into a substantial and ethical source of passive income:

Creating Valuable and Honest Content:

- Niche Focus: Nikhil selected a niche that not only aligned with his expertise and interests but also allowed him to contribute valuable and truthful insights to his audience.

- Quality and Transparency: He committed to publishing high-quality, honest content consistently, ensuring that his readers could trust the information and recommendations provided on his blog.

Building an Audience with Integrity:

- Ethical Promotion Strategies: Nikhil utilized transparent social media practices, SEO, and genuine networking to drive traffic to his blog. He engaged with his audience in an open and honest manner, building trust and credibility.
- Community Engagement: By actively interacting with readers through comments and social media, Nikhil fostered a loyal and trusting community that appreciated his commitment to honesty and integrity.

Monetizing the Blog with Integrity:

- Ethical Income Streams: Nikhil carefully explored monetization strategies that aligned with his values, such as affiliate marketing, sponsored posts, and advertising, ensuring that all partnerships were with brands he genuinely trusted and believed in.
- Honest Partnerships: He formed strategic partnerships with companies that shared his

ethical standards, creating opportunities for transparent sponsored content and product reviews that provided real value to his readers.

Continuous Learning and Ethical Adaptation:

- Skill Development: Nikhil invested time in learning about digital marketing, SEO, and ethical monetization techniques. He attended webinars and read industry publications to stay updated on best practices while maintaining his commitment to honesty.

- Adapting with Integrity: He regularly analysed his blog's performance and adapted his strategies based on reader feedback, ensuring that all changes aligned with his core values of honesty and ethical practice.

Results: Nikhil's dedication to earning money through honest means led to impressive results:

- Significant Passive Income: His blog became a reliable source of passive income, generating substantial revenue through ethical and transparent income streams.

- Professional Growth: Nikhil's expertise in ethical blogging and digital marketing opened new professional opportunities, including consulting and speaking engagements where he could share his values-driven approach.

- Personal Fulfillment: The success of his blog provided personal satisfaction and a deep sense of accomplishment, reaffirming his decision to pursue his passion with integrity.

Nikhil's journey exemplifies the importance of 'Earning Through Honest Means.' His success demonstrates that with determination, continuous learning, and a commitment to ethical practices, it is possible to turn a passion project into a significant source of passive income. Nikhil's story illustrates that honesty, perseverance, and the willingness to adapt are essential for achieving long-term success in any endeavour.

Reflections!

'Mortal Morals' brings forward the hidden connection between personal ideals and aspiration of financial freedom. The book demystifies the path to financial well-being by first looking into mind, within self on morals; our values impacting everything we do in life, from money to emotional, relationships and so much more – physically growing into the person that we become.

Key Themes and Insights

The Foundation of Morals:

- Your core values can affect your money life. In order to make ethical financial choices, you must first understand your own moral compass.

Morals and Financial well-being:

- Aligning Values with Financial Goals: Financial well-being is not just about becoming rich; it's about developing a strategy to reach your life's goals. 'Mortal Morals' states that one can be truly financially independent when life's goals can be achieved by factoring in ethical principles.
- Ethical Wealth Creation: Learn how ethical values can help with the creation and management of

wealth. The book explains why achieving financial success through ethically-moral practices results in a fulfilling and sustainable independence.

Morals and Emotional Well-Being:

- Finding Internal Harmony – The book talks about why and how making your money life congruent with your value system leads to less stress, greater emotional happiness and a feeling of "this is enough" rather than striving for material goals alone.

Relationships and Morals:

- Impacts on Personal Relationships: Understand how your values affect the way you relate to people in personal and business life. Making ethical choices can often facilitate stronger relationships and consequently further business opportunities.
- Networking and Collaboration: The book also points out how moral values can impact the networking and professional collaborations one does and how being ethical in these areas can actually enable professionals to create more meaningful and productive relationship.

Growth and Self-Reflection:

- Evolving Morals: Morals are not static, and they can change as you grow through life. 'Mortal

Morals' is all about constantly self-reflecting and re-evaluating what's important to you while reaching for FIRE.

- Increasing the Depth of You Understanding: They discuss how situational factors can influence your moral perspectives and the importance of striking a balance between flexibility and consistency in your beliefs.

Case Study

Deepali's Journey to a Robust Retirement Fund

Deepali, a 40-year-old accountant, had realised the significance of planning for her retirement early on in her career. Having started with modest savings at the beginning, she was clear right from the start that she would have to accumulate a sizeable corpus over the years. Deepali believes in being "Consistent and Wise Investing".

Challenge: Deepali's main challenges were:

- Starting with a Small Amount: She had only a modest amount to contribute initially, and it was hard to imagine how that could become anything of real scale anytime soon.
- 2. Maintaining Consistency: It took discipline to keep making contributions regularly while still managing my day-to-day expenses and other financial obligations.
- Choosing Smart Investments: How she would need to make her money work for her over time in order to grow her savings.

Solution: Deepali's retirement savings' success story was the case of "Consistency and Wise Investing", which she carried all along her retirement savings journey. And here's how she could grow it big:

Starting Small but Steadily:

- Initial Contributions: Deepali started with a small monthly contribution to her retirement account that she could easily manage. The small start didn't matter. It was important to get started.
- Automate your savings: Deepali started auto deductions in her pay check to be transferred to her retirement account, it was an easy set it and forget way of saving money.

Maintaining Discipline:

- It really mattered to Deepali that she had made it a point to increase her contributions every time she had a raise in salary or any windfall gains, using and following the disciplined approach towards savings.
- Budget Management: She was very careful to keep her expenses low and make sure that saving for retirement was a priority, even as other costs fluctuated.

Smart Investment Choices:

- Diversified Portfolio: Deepali educated herself about different types of investments and then built a diversified portfolio which was a good balance between risk and potential returns. This was on the foundations of shares, bonds as well as mutual funds.

- Regular Reviews: She met with her financial advisor periodically to review and adjust her investment strategy if needed based on market conditions or changes in her own financial situation and goals to make sure she was still on track.

Long-Term Focus:

- Compounding Growth: Deepali was very clear about the power of compounding, and hence she was patient. She knew that over a long term, your own savings start earning for you, provided you keep contributing regularly & invest wisely.
- Staying Informed: She kept herself updated with the market trends and financial planning, which helped her take right decisions with her retirement fund.

Impact: Deepali's retirement corpus built up over the years, resulting in:

- Substantial Growth: Her consistent contributions and strategic investments led to substantial growth of her retirement savings providing for a strong financial cushion in the future.
- Financial Security: Deepali had made sure with her disciplined approach and wise investments to create a strong retirement fund. And this used to give her the peace of mind that her financial future is secured.

- Empowerment: The success of her savings plans gave Deepali the confidence to plan for retirement and work on other financial goals, knowing she was starting from a solid foundation.

'Consistency and Wise Investing' is what Deepali's story is all about. It goes on to prove that even a small and consistent investing over a long period coupled with wise investment choices can lead to good corpus. Her disciplined approach in taking decisions speaks volumes of how this attitude coupled with some planning can help achieve your financial goals.

Results from Market Research

To back my observations and learnings, I surveyed more than 800 people and here's what we were able to analyse.

The survey data reveals in depth insights of the ethics and values of the respondents, bifurcated among different demographics like age, profession, annual income etc. A detailed report which summaries the findings is as follows:

Total Respondents: 829 - The dataset includes a varied range of participants with diverse backgrounds.

Top Morals Identified

Across all respondents, certain morals were consistently highlighted as important:

Most Common Morals:

- Honesty
- Kindness
- Respect
- Hard Work
- Discipline
- Compassion

The morals were chosen again and again across many demographic groups, indicating that these particular morals are of strong and possibly universal importance.

Morals by Age Group

- Younger Age Group (20-30 years):
  - Predominant Morals: Hard Work, Discipline, Respect

  This age-group focuses more on morals related to the personal and professional life because they are at the stage where they have to make their career.

- Middle Age Group (31-50 years):
  - Predominant Morals: Honesty, Kindness, Responsibility

  This kind of people mainly think highly of integrity and social harmonious, so they often need to take the role of taking care of family as well as work.

- Older Age Group (51+ years):
  - Predominant Morals: Compassion, Fairness, Patience

  Older respondents focused on morals that were more connected to wisdom and focused on relationships and the kind of legacy that you leave.

Morals by Education Level

- High School Graduates:
  - Focus on Discipline and Hard Work — morals that are forced into again and again during their course of education.

- College Graduates:
    - Honesty and Responsibility should be the main points that I would like to highline in my life, it would be either private or business life.
- Post-Graduates:
    - Value Compassion and Fairness-it could be due to increased exposure and higher education which results in a broader perspective on the world.

Morals by Profession

- Salaried Employees:
    - Common Morals: Hard Work, Honesty, Discipline

    The ethics most conducive to high performance and dependability tend to be prized by those undergoing that experience.
- Self-Employed Individuals:
    - Common Morals: Responsibility, Fairness, Innovation

    Responsibility and fairness. Entrepreneurs as well as freelancers know that these two qualities are essential if you want to maintain business relationship and innovate for growth.

- Professionals:
    - Common Morals: Integrity, Respect, Compassion

  Leadership individuals especially emphasize morals intended to facilitate trust and respectful relations.

Influence of Mentors and Self-Learning

- Impact of Mentors:

  It is clear from the data that respondents with mentors often rate Integrity and Responsibility higher, indicating that mentorship cultivates these values.

- Investment in Self-Learning:

  Those who invest in self-learning, I see a strong dominance of the morals like Innovation and Discipline, probably because they keep working on themselves.

Importance of Honesty and Hard Work

- Honesty: Universally viewed as the most important core value across all ages, income brackets and professions – indicating that honesty is considered a fundamental moral value by everyone.
- Hard Work: Especially stressed by younger participants and those at an early career stage, indicating possible importance for 'making it'.

Morals by Income Level

- Lower Income Bracket (<5 LPA):
  - It implicitly tells you that work and discipline are keys to making it up the ladder.
- Middle Income Bracket (5-20 LPA):
  - Focus on Honesty and Respect, the core values of harmony, describes their determination to growing financially.
- Higher Income Bracket (>20 LPA):
  - Focus on Responsibility and Compassion, maybe because of the larger impact and focus on returning to the society.

Influential People in Life

Respondents were also asked which one group of people have the most influence over how they think about right and wrong and the values and moral standards by which they live–including their views about money.

Key Findings:

- Parents: The most commonly reported influential group across all ages.

  Impact: Respondents who were influenced by their parents, tend to hold traditional values such as Honesty, Respect and Responsibility at high regard, and may be more likely to adopt conservative financial strategies that emphasizes on stability and security.

- School Friends:
  - Younger Respondents (20-30 years): Most important for younger respondents, illustrating the likely impact of peer effects during one's formative years.

  Impact: This segment is more inclined towards Hard Work and Discipline as they are in or starting their early careers. They might experiment more with their money and be influenced by peer trends.

- Bosses/Mentors:
  - Middle Age Group (31-50 years): Interning becomes a vague memory now. You are actually growing in your job, and bosses/ mentors start having to put in extra efforts to keep you inspired.

  Impact: Values such as Integrity, Professionalism and Fairness are emphasized. Financial decisions in this group might be more strategic, with a focus on long term growth and ethical practices.

- Spouse/Partner: There were some respondents who said that their partner were influential for their life.

  Impact: This cluster frequently listed Compassion and Teamwork as important values, and shared a view on financial planning and life. Financial plans are often 'we' strategies that typically include plans to mutual benefit or allocated responsibility.

- Religious Leaders/Community Figures:
  - Older Age Group (51+ years): This was the most significant for older respondents specifically, highlighting the need for moral and ethical role modelling in later stages of life.

  Impact: Values like Compassion, Generosity, Patience etc. Personally, I have seen people taking financial decisions which are more for the sake of community good, giving back or ethical investing etc.

Investment in Self-Learning

It's an important key to personal and financial growth.

Key Findings:

- Overall Investment:
  - Over half of the respondents had invested in self-learning, which implied the kind of interest people have for personal improvement and continuous development.
- By Age Group:
  - Younger Age Group (20-30 years): High self-learning investment. This group is proactively

looking for skill and knowledge building to escalate their professional graph.

Impact: They are likely to value Innovation and Adaptability, and thus have more of dynamic financial strategies (such as investing in new opportunities/start-ups).

- Middle Age Group (31-50 years): Kept on learning but most of the times the emphasis was self-learning, it was more of on professional front and on leadership.

Impact: Values such as Professionalism and Strategic Thinking dominate. Financial decisions might include taking more calculated risks, and diversifying one's portfolio.

- Older Age Group (51+ years): Lesser yet significant investment in self-learning often related to hobbies, retirement planning or new life stages.

Impact: Values such as Wisdom and Contentment are emphasized, with financial decisions often with regard to security and legacy planning.

- By Profession:
  - Salaried Employees: They invest a lot in self-learning, primarily because they have to stay competitive in their careers.

Impact: This group may have financial decisions such as saving more for future education, or a professional certification.

- Self-Employed: Invest in self-learning as well regarding entrepreneurial skills and market trends.

Impact: They value Innovation and Resilience, often leading to riskier but potentially high-reward financial strategies.

- Professionals should keep investing on self-learning's specially in the areas which add on to the leadership and strategic decision making.

Impact: Because they are usually either mainly motivated or secondarily motivated by economic or financial factors, this means their financial strategies are generally very conservative as well as being knowledgeable and aimed at long-term sustainability.

Correlation Between Influential People and Self-Learning

- Mentors/Bosses: Respondents who indicated their boss or a mentor as one of the biggest influences on their continued to take their self-education seriously were more likely to take up learning opportunities overall, suggesting a link between having strong role models in your working life and a desire to strive for constant improvement.

- Parents and Self-Learning: Those who were influenced by parents, they told them to start self-learning things early on in life and kept telling them that education never stops, and that education has an impact on how much money you make.

Conclusions

This survey examines the intricate relationship between personal moral convictions and variables such as upbringing, education, and wealth, and reveals how these convictions can be mediated and modified in the process.

Morals and Upbringing

Influence of Family Values:

- Primary Factor: The survey shows that the family is the main factor to impact forming individual's moral. Normally, when we were child, our parent taught us how to distinguish between right and wrong so that at the beginning of life, people know why they should not do some harmful activities.
- Variations by Background: People are likely to have divergent moral beliefs owning to the

fact that they were brought up in different family backgrounds. For example, those who were born and grew up in a rather rigorous and conventional family are more likely to embrace conservative perspectives, while others who were raised in liberal families would possibly take on some progressive views.

Parenting Styles:

- Authority vs. acceptance: The study finds that parents' authoritative style, which combines warmth with rules and guidance, fosters a clear-cut sense of right and wrong in kids. Parents' permissive style, providing little more than nurturance, tends to promote a less defined and less stringent morality.

Morals and Education

- Educational Impact:
    - Exposure to Diverse Perspectives: Higher levels of education typically expose people to a wider array of perspectives and ethical quandaries. This exposure can produce a more sophisticated understanding of morality that is inclusive of multiple points-of-view.
    - Critical Thinking Skills: Education helps in developing critical thinking skills in an individual. People with higher educational qualification are more likely to have better

and broader mind-sets as compared to those with lower qualifications. They tend to raise their morals on account of the general principles being adopted by people with higher qualifications

- Moral Development:
  - Formal Education: Study reveals that formal education contributes to moral development as it stimulates ethical reasoning and empathy. Moral and ethical issues are included in school/college curriculum at times which could have impacts on the morality of students.

Morals and Financial Situations

- Economic Influences:
  - Income and Ethical Choices: The survey does not reveal whether people in different income brackets actually do have different moral priorities. For example, it could be the case that higher-income people should have different moral concerns but nonetheless don't.
- Financial Security and Moral Flexibility:
  - Economic Stability: Financial stability can affect moral flexibility. Those with higher income might have lower financial pressure which guarantees the freedom to stick to their original moral choices or change their moral

choices based on normative convictions not for economic concerns.

Morals are Malleable

- Situational Influences:
    - The survey brings to light the fact that morals are not rigid but flexible and can change with the times. People often re-evaluate their moral values in case of any major changes in life situations such as, a change of profession, personal relationships or due to some socio-economic changes.
- Contextual Flexibility:
    - The results imply that people tend to adapt their moral mind-sets depending on the context they are in. That is, one might think and feel differently about moral matters at the workplace than in one's private sphere, indicating that situational contexts impact on moral judgement.

The Role of Mentors

How Mentors Can Help Align Morals and Money Goals

There are instances when making money will put us in a position where our judgments about right and wrong are tested as we proceed on our journey to be good at it. This could be hard, especially in times when making money tends to cloud off important values with temptation. That is why mentors are very important. A mentor is not just a financial planning adviser; he is a knowledgeable person who would help you feel the connection between your money goals and values.

Mentors have a lot of experience, which can really light the way for you. They usually have dealt with the problems that you have faced and can share tips on how to handle them without losing your values. A good mentor will help you understand the big picture; making money is not all about getting rich but getting rich in a manner that reflects who you really are.

One of the key duties of a mentor is to listen and provide advice. When you have tough choices that clash between making money and sticking with morals, a mentor will help you see things more clearly. Hence, they will make you think of options that you are not likely to see, letting you achieve your goals in money while holding your values.

They will also want you to stay true to your values when things go wrong. They will remind you that quick wins from bending your morals can lead to a really unhappy, sorry you in the future. By keeping you focused, mentors will help you to create a financial legacy that you can be proud of—one that will work out who you really are.

Finding mentors who share your moral values

Picking the right mentor is very important to make sure your money journey matches your values. A mentor can have a strong effect on you, so it's necessary to choose someone who knows about money plans and also shares or respects your beliefs.

First work out what is important to you in life and in your money journey. Are you interested in ethical investing, clear business practices, or maybe sharing wealth generously? Find mentors who live according to them. Once you know what your values are, find mentors who live according to them. This match is so important because it ensures the advice you get will align with what you really believe. A mentor who has consistently showed a high level of commitment to their morals about financial matters will likely give advice in line with your values.

You may find them at professional events for networking, in professional groups, or through personal referrals. But don't rush. This type of relationship grows with time and must be built on mutual respect, shared values, etc. Talk about things other than strategies for making or managing money; life concepts, ethical dilemmas, the role of values in making financial decisions, etc. All this will help you to gauge if the potential mentor has the values that would be very close to your own.

You don't always need to see a person face-to-face to have a mentor. Books, podcasts, and online courses by smart people with similar values can help you learn, too. What matters is that the advice you get helps you make money choices that square with your beliefs.

The Effect of Mentorship on Long-Term Money Health

There are many ways a mentor can help you—not just giving you advice about money. Over the long term, having a mentor will have a greater effect on your financial health because you are guided through your decisions to ones that match your values.

One of the greatest benefits accruing from having a mentor is building financial strength. With a mentor who helps you support your values, you are likely to make choices that you can easily believe in, even through hard times. This clearly becomes the most essential kind of strength in ensuring lifetime success in finance, since one will avoid making decisions that could reach the heights of being shortsighted.

Additionally, mentors help you keep the prize in your eyes of your long-term vision. The easily skewed road to financial well-being is offset by short-term chances that may not go along with your belief system. A mentor reminds you of the bigger picture and helps you think through the possible benefits versus the moral costs. This puts a very important long-term view in creating something lasting in the financial future.

Mentorship keeps you learning and growing as an individual. The path of money will morph, and the challenges will shift. A mentor will help support and guide you through new situations while allowing you to remain loyal to the values you held before. Staying synced between your morals and financial goals ensures that financial health is secured not as a short-term win, but for lasting gains.

Also, the relationship you develop with a mentor surpasses financial constraints. A mentor can shape your outlook on life, inspire you to achieve not just material success but also balance and a sense of purpose in your life that is respectful of your values. This holistic approach to mentoring furthers your well-being and helps make sure that your financial success adds to, rather than takes away from, your quality of life. In conclusion, the role of financial mentors in one's life achievement is very immense. These people help you relate your financial objectives with moral values and, through that, they ensure whatever you achieve in life happens to be rich and right. Mentors influence how you make your financial choices—directly or by example—all the way through creating a good wealth legacy you can use throughout your life.

Are you ready to take the next step toward your moral financial well-being? Discover how mentorship can help you achieve your goals with a complimentary session. Let's explore if we're the right fit to work together on your journey to success. Book your free discovery call today, and let's see how we can turn your aspirations into reality You can visit www.uplift-india.com, if you wish to discuss getting mentored.

To discuss about the learnings of this book, log on to www.mortalmorals.in and join the MM Community.

Practical Applications

Case Studies and Examples

This book uses the market research's outcomes to present how people with different understandings differently go through their finances while staying in line with what they believe to be right.

Personal Development

We've explored the intersection of morality and financial freedom, and how our most fundamental beliefs influence both our money choices and personal development. The book started with a detailed examination into moral values and illustrated how when we make these values the cornerstones of our financial practices, we not only generate ethical wealth but also enjoy greater well-being. It presented a road map for integrating the often-neglected moral dimensions of life into our financial blueprint and shared actionable strategies to achieve economic security without compromising inner peace and personal fulfillment. Ultimately, it made clear that true wealth involves much more than just acquiring monetary riches; it entails living a value-centered life.

Recognize that morals are not fixed but can be newly crafted or adapted to align with your financial goals. Moreover, pick on role models whose morals you want to adapt, and adapt them!

If you find yourself feeling stuck, identify which moral principle might be hindering your progress. This reflection can reveal actionable pathways to reinvent yourself and reshape your journey towards financial well-being.

I wish you all the best in causing your financial well-being!

"Be yourself; everyone else is already taken." — Oscar Wilde

Thank You!

Thank you for joining me on this insightful journey through Mortal Morals. This book explores the powerful connection between personal values and financial well-being. By delving deeply into your morals, it makes the path to financial well-being clearer and more ethical.

In these pages, you would have discovered how your values shape your financial decisions, influence your emotional health, and affect your relationships. This guidance aims to help you achieve financial well-being in a way that is both balanced and fulfilling.

I'm truly honoured that you chose to embark on this journey with me. Your support means the world, and I look forward to sharing more insights and discoveries with you in the future.

Thank you for being a part of this incredible journey!

"It is not the strongest of the species that survive, nor the most intelligent, but the one most responsive to change."

— Charles Darwin

Acknowledgements

First and foremost, I express my deepest gratitude to God, the universal energy that flows through every aspect of life, guiding, nurturing, and illuminating the path of discovery and growth.

To my wife, Komal—your unwavering support, love, and belief in me have been the bedrock of my journey. Your presence has been a source of strength, allowing me to pursue my passion with courage and conviction.

To my friends and family, your encouragement, wisdom, and companionship have been invaluable. You've cheered me on through every challenge and celebrated each victory with me. Thank you for being my pillars of strength and joy.

To my mentees, who have allowed me the privilege of being a part of their journeys—I've grown alongside you as a coach and mentor. Your trust and willingness to learn have pushed me to continuously evolve and expand my own understanding.

To the mentors who have guided me, your insights and teachings have shaped my path in profound ways. Your wisdom has been a beacon, lighting the way through the complexities of life and helping me to see new possibilities.

A special thanks to the teams at Landmark Education and Passionpreneur—your programs have been instrumental in my self-learning and growth. The lessons I've learned through your guidance have been transformative, helping me to unlock new potentials and deepen my understanding of myself and the world.

Lastly, I am deeply grateful for life itself. Every moment is a teacher, every experience an opportunity for growth. The continuous flow of learning and transformation has enriched my journey and made it a truly rewarding experience.

This book is a culmination of all these influences, and I'm humbled by the support and love that has brought me to this point. Thank you to everyone who has been a part of this incredible journey. Your influence, support, and love are woven into every page of this book.

"The chains of habit are too light to be felt until they are too heavy to be broken."

"Do not save what is left after spending, but spend what is left after saving."

— Warren Buffett

www.ingramcontent.com/pod-product-compliance
Ingram Content Group UK Ltd.
Pitfield, Milton Keynes, MK11 3LW, UK
UKHW022020041026
15591UKWH00012B/394

9 798895 448441